THE HOUSE
WITHOUT DOORS

By

DANELLE WRIGHT

Copyright © 2022 by Danelle Wright

All rights reserved. No part of this publication may be reproduced, stored in any form of retrieval system or transmitted in any form or by any means without prior permission in writing from the publishers except for the use of brief quotations in a book review.

ISBN (Hardback): 979-8-9860160-0-9

Book production by MysticqueRose Publishing Services LLC

Contents

Fatherlessness in the World Today iv

1. So This Is Life on Earth 6
2. Who's talking to me? 15
3. If You Tell, You'll Regret It 20
4. You Just Don't Belong, Little Momma 26
5. Seen but Not Seen 36
6. Who Said Women Don't Sexually Abuse Children? 47
7. Finding A Way to Fit In 57
8. So You Think You're Grown 66
9. It's Better to Marry than to Burn 76
10. From the Pot to the Frying Pan 86
11. I've Healed Too Much to Let You Keep Beating Me 96
12. Living Life after Abuse 118

Foreword

Fatherlessness in the World Today

While I was growing up, I thought of fathers as the disciplinarians in the home. Fathers are traditionally seen as the providers and protectors of their families, and I never met a friend who wanted to hear their mother say,

"I'm going to tell your father when he gets home."

All my friends who had fathers would rather get disciplined by their mother on the spot than risk whatever their father would have in store for them when he got home. Yet, I envied them, especially those who had both parents intact. They had two loving parents in their lives who would pour out all of their love for them. From my perspective, they always seemed happier than I was. Their families seemed more stable and seemed to have better relationships with each other. Everyone seemed so close. They had more money, went on vacations, had beautiful name-brand clothes, had more toys and were more confident than the rest of us.

These are just some of the consequences I witnessed firsthand growing up without a father.

Not having a father in my home affected my life as a child and in adulthood. I can admit now that I fell into multiple statistics and stereotypes of children without fathers. After having my own unenviable experience of growing up without a father, I found myself raising my kids without an active, loving father of their own—a void that also greatly affected them. Statistics show that we have a serious crisis on our hands; one that far outweighs the current pandemic. Without a doubt, something has to be done or the future will look worse.

With this book, I aim to bring awareness to the devastation of fatherlessness and help those that may have been affected by the absence of their husbands in their children's lives. This book also addresses heartbreak, abuse, purpose, and healing. If you seek deliverance from bondage, I encourage you to join me on this journey as I share my story. Join me as I dive into the most intimate parts of my life. Join me as I expose my fears, scars, and the spiritual journey towards loving myself and appreciating all I had to endure. I am incomplete without my story. It is what made me who I am today, and with it, I encourage you to break the bondage and live your best life!

Chapter 1

So This Is Life on Earth

The late 50s welcomed both my parents into the small town of Fresno, California. Although they were born and raised in Fresno, neither were natives. Both sides of my family had migrated from the south to Fresno, a town known for its agriculture and was seen as a place that would offer them better opportunities.

Fresno was a family town at the time. Most of its occupants practiced Christianity, and many of its minorities worked the fields, toiled on train tracks, picked crops, and managed any other low-wage jobs they could find. While it was not the south, it still had the familiar stench of oppression and inequality. So, it became common for the poor to look out for each other and know everyone in the neighborhood.

My mother's father was exceptionally skilled at farming and gardening. I grew up following him to auctions where he sold the hogs he had painstakingly raised. He was a devoted family man whose upbringing helped secure his strong values.

As the oldest boy of eleven children, my grandfather was forced to drop out of school in the 3rd grade to work with his father to support the family. Over the years, he would grow into a large man, who wasn't particularly tall but could eat an entire chicken by himself for dinner. My grandfather sang, cooked, preached, told funny jokes, and was honestly blunt. He had been a chef in an upscale restaurant before opening a home for the elderly that he cared for until he retired. He did all of this while pastoring and still managed to be involved in the life of his wife, children, and grandchildren. It was nearly impossible to see him without one of us.

My maternal grandmother was the only child of a couple who left her in the care of her grandparents and moved to California in search of more opportunities. However, things went sour, they divorced but her mother sent for her. There, she met my grandfather. They went to church together and quickly became friends. Before asking for my grandmother's hand in marriage, my grandfather bought a car and a home. Together, they had six children; five girls and a boy. My mother was the second oldest.

My parents might have been high school sweethearts, but they were completely different.

My mother was a beautiful woman in every sense of the word. Her five-foot-five slender frame was graced by smooth ebony skin. Her hair was black, pressed and curled, and so long that she often needed help rolling it at night because her arms couldn't stretch far enough to reach its ends. She walked so gracefully that she seemed to float, leaving behind a luscious fragrance in the air from her designer perfume. She attracted attention from men every time my brother and I went out with her. They would whistle and comment on her beauty, but my mother was sophisticated enough to ignore them. Their words weren't worth her attention and she carried herself in that fashion. She had always been a smart, focused, and confident woman who, in high school, kept good grades while working part-time for the local OB-GYN that her mother also worked for.

My father was also a beautiful man: he had a fair complexion, high cheekbones, and a perfectly picked-out afro. He was about five foot eleven and played the quarterback position on the high school football team. However, while my mother carried herself with grace, ignoring men's advances, my father enjoyed being the bad boy that all the girls wanted.

My mother had had a sheltered upbringing under strict, religious parents. My father, on the other hand, grew up with a mother and stepfather that drank, partied, and never went to church. He wasn't the choice my grandparents would have made for their daughter, but they were in love and immediately had my older brother and me after marrying straight out of high school.

Religion was compulsory in my mother's family. Her parents forced them to go to church multiple times per week. There were stories about how, for the smallest things, my grandmother would beat my mom and her siblings until they bled. Unsurprisingly, my mom grew to hate her, and the coerced church attendance deepened the resentment. My grandmother had this habit of forcing her children to go up to the altar to pray for the Holy Ghost at every service. On one of those nights, my mother said she prayed to God. She told Him that she wasn't sure if He was real but assured Him that if her mother forced her to go up the altar that night, she would curse Him.

Surprisingly, her mother did not force them to go up to the altar. Later that night, while they were all in the car on the way home, my grandmother said that God had spoken to her during the service. He had instructed my grandmother not to force her children up the altar because one of them had threatened to curse Him. And if they did, He would certainly kill them.

My mother sank in her seat. She told us that it was at that moment that she knew God was real.

However, this event did nothing to improve the relationship between my mother and grandmother. It only caused her to get married quickly, right out of high school. However, she still saw life through the lens of the church and her parents. She had never been exposed to drugs or domestic abuse. Her father had never raised a hand to hit his wife, and my mother never saw her father with another woman, so my mother never imagined she would have to endure any of that when she got married.

Meanwhile, my father remained a lady's man. He got a good job, rode a motorcycle, and basked in the following attention. He'd never had a responsible father figure. His biological father had been absent, and his stepfather had no values or morals to impart. His biological father also had a quick temper, and my mother told us that he had mercilessly beaten my father with a water hose at some point in his life. However, my father still doted on his mother even though she'd been no better than his father. She was an in-house prostitute who spent her time drinking one-fifth of Old Granddad bourbon every day. However, she'd spoiled my father because he was her only child. So, he grew up with the impression that he could do no wrong.

Still, he knew what my mother's parents had, and he admired it. He wanted it for his family. He even tried to be a part of the church by joining the choir. However, after a choir rehearsal, one of the brothers publicly embarrassed him, after catching him smoking outside the church premises. The humiliation and judgment he suffered due to that act caused him to leave the church and never return.

At home, the situation was less bleak. In the beginning, my parent's marriage was blissful. They bought a house, made a home, and hosted hangouts with their family and friends. My dad loved my brother and me. I was a daddy's girl. My mom told me a story that proved just how true this was.

There was a time when my parents were entertaining guests in their garage. They had transformed the garage into a lounge. It had a pool table and everything else you would find in a well-designed lounge. There was a big stereo in the living room that was loud enough to serenade them within the house and outside. It was one of those days when they were serenading when suddenly it stopped. My father walked into the living room to check the stereo only to find me wrapped up in the tape. My little self had opened the player and pulled the tape out, tangling myself in the process. Naturally, he was pissed, so he yelled at me. And naturally, I was frightened, so I started crying, but he was so affected by my response that he also started crying and had to tell my mother to get me.

Ultimately, my parents started responsibly. They were homeowners who had life insurance policies and a trust fund set up for my brother and me for when we turned 23. But, the burden of early marriage, the responsibility of having children without sorting through their separate childhood traumas, and the differences in their backgrounds proved to be the perfect recipe for disaster. Predictably, the temptation of being with other women was difficult for my father to resist. My mother had to endure his infidelity, the STDs he gave her, and being the laughingstock of the town because my father had no shame.

At the time, they both worked for the Post Office. One night, two women got into a fight over my father right in front of my mother's desk. Another time, she came home to find my father sitting on the couch in the living room with a lady dancing over him, holding my mother's priceless wedding champagne glass.

The moment my mother confronted them, the lady ran out the front door, and my father ran after her, yelling back at my mom, "Look what you did!"

However, my mother was not the only one who had to suffer from my father's escapades. I also had my fair share. Before I turned a year old, I got diarrhea so bad that my body suffered from dehydration. My mom told me that even though I had only had it for a few hours when she rushed me to the ER, it didn't take long for dehydration to set in. My soft spot sunk in, and my skin turned gray. My mom said the doctors struggled to get an IV into me because my veins couldn't handle it. Eventually, the doctors gave up. There was nothing else they could do. Meanwhile, my father had run off with another woman.

When it seemed like all hope was lost, my mother gave my frail body to her mother, went home, and slept on her knees, praying. She said she could not stand to watch me die. My grandmother stayed with me all night, praying, as she fed me a Jell-O mix out of my bottle. She promised God that if He spared my life, she would make it her responsibility to teach me about Him and raise me to serve Him. My grandmother was a pediatric nurse and was familiar with the tragic sight of seeing infants die. A week before I got sick, another baby suffering from diarrhea, the same illness I was battling, had been rushed in by her parents. The child wasn't as dehydrated as I was, yet died within hours.

Thankfully, I survived through the night. So, my grandmother asked the doctors to insert the IV one more time. They hesitated. They reminded her that my veins couldn't handle it. They had even shaved my head and tried to insert an IV there, and it still didn't work. But my grandmother begged them to try again. This time, she requested for them to do a cutdown on my ankle to access the main artery. They agreed to satisfy her request but were confident that it wouldn't save my life. They were just waiting for me to die, but God touched my body and healed me completely. Since that day, my grandmother never stopped sharing that testimony in church and I still wear the scar on my inner left ankle.

Back at home, my parents' marriage was headed for the rocks. It was crumbling and had gotten to the point where nothing could hold it together. Not their good intentions, nor the love they had for each other, and not even their love for us. Eventually, my father had to move out. Then, my mother found out she was pregnant with their third child. With her marriage on the rocks, she felt the best thing to do was get rid of the baby. She did. Then, a week after her abortion, a tragedy would strike.

On a fishing trip with some friends, my father had a terrible car accident in which his car flipped multiple times. His friends were able to get out of the vehicle safely but he was pinned down by the steering wheel. The car caught fire and his friends watched helplessly as he was burned alive. By the time he was taken to the hospital, he was still alive but his entire body was burned except his face and head. Unfortunately, the injuries he sustained were too severe and he died at the age of 23.

My grandfather had a saying that went like this, "How you lived will be seen at your funeral." This saying couldn't have been more fitting for any man than my father because his funeral was a perfect display of how he'd lived his life. My mom said there were so many women crying over his casket that she, his wife, didn't even feel comfortable crying. She also noticed a Hispanic woman at my dad's funeral that sat in the back, didn't say anything to anyone, and left before anyone could say anything to her.

Who was this woman? There had been rumors that the woman that raised my father was not his biological mother, but she had always denied it. She was very dark and my father was very light so many people believed the rumors. It wasn't until after he died that my dad's father told me that my real grandmother was a lady named Maria Valdez from Mexico. By the time he told me the truth, Maria had died. I never got to know anything about her or her family. She was just another mistress of my grandfather's who had gotten pregnant. When she delivered my father, she abandoned him in the hospital and listed my grandfather as the father but left no information about herself. My grandfather picked up my dad from the hospital, and since he was married, he ended up giving my father to another mistress of his, who couldn't have children. The woman that raised him was named Lori.

Lori was tall, thin, and dark with big lips. She was a wild woman. She owned a home and raised chickens on the West side of town where the majority of the minorities lived. She always sat in her old, yellow and green, flower-decorated recliner daily, facing her front door with a pistol under the seat cushion and she was not afraid to use it. She married after taking custody of my father. Her husband was a nice, gentle man. He loved her and my father. He was so heartbroken after my father died, that he didn't last much longer afterward. Lori and my grandfather didn't maintain a cordial relationship. Not once did I ever see him visit Lori's house.

There is no doubt that my parent's background played a major role in the lives they lived as adults. They were too immature to handle the responsibilities they signed up for, so they ended up hurting each other. My mother became a young widow with two children aged three and one. She lost the only man she had ever loved. If she had known that he was going to die, would she have gotten the abortion? The trauma she endured in her marriage and from the tragic loss of her husband would add to the wounds she already had. But she came from a long line of strong black women, and she was not about to give up.

Psalm 68:5

"Father of the fatherless and protector of the widows is God in his holy habitation."

Chapter 2

Who's talking to me?

After my father died, we continued living in the three-bedroom home he and my mother bought. Her older sister also decided to move in with us to ease the burden off my mom.

My aunt shared a story with me about the time she spent living with us and why she left. She told me that one day, while she was taking a shower, the bathroom door opened, and she could see someone walk in. The shower door was foggy, and all my aunt could see was a shadowy figure taking a seat on the toilet. So, she immediately assumed it was my mom and began talking to her. Shortly after she began the conversation, the shadow stood, walked out, and the door closed behind it. Thinking my mom had walked out on her in the middle of their conversation, my aunt got offended and got out of the shower to scold her younger sister. To her surprise, my mom told her that she wasn't the one who had walked into the bathroom.

The experience was eerie for my aunt, but she did her best to shake it off with some logical explanation. This 'logical explanation' fell apart when she had her next encounter.

This time, she was in the living room when she heard the sound of our silverware drawer open and the clattering noise of utensils falling to the floor. Immediately, she ran to the kitchen but found that there was nothing there. Not a single fork was on the floor. She remembered that my mom told her not to worry if she heard noises or if strange things happened because it was my father, and she had been aware for a while that his spirit was still in the house. She also told my aunt that sometimes, while she was in bed, she could feel the bed sink as he sat on its edge next to her. This information and experience were too much for my aunt to bear. She packed her belongings, left that day, and never came back.

I was not without my own experiences with my father after his death. My mother told me that at the tender age of two before I could grasp the concept of lying, I would hold out my lollipop while playing and snatch it back as if I was letting someone lick it then fall out laughing. When I was asked who I was playing with, my little self would say, "My Daddy."

These events continued for years, and my mother's religious family were strongly against it as they believed I was communicating with the dead. I remember one scripture, in particular, that was used to "prove" that it wasn't my father I was speaking to. It was Ecclesiastes 9:5-6, which states:

For the living know that they shall die: but the dead know not any thing, neither have they any more reward; for the memory of them is forgotten. Also their love, and their hatred, and their envy, is now perished; neither have they any more portion for ever in anything that is done under the sun.

Because of this belief, some of my family members even refused to babysit me because they thought my father's spirit would follow them. So, I was taught that since the dead had no knowledge of the living, there was no way it could be my father, and it was probably a demonic spirit. Unsurprisingly, fear began to set in. I grew up thinking there was something wrong with me. I was ashamed, I grew scared, and I was terrified. I began to fear all dead people.

I remember not being able to sleep alone. My older brother would allow me to sleep with him because I started having nightmares of deceased family members appearing to me. After a family member would die, I wouldn't even be able to muster up the courage to go to the bathroom alone because, to me, it looked like a casket.

When I was about seven years old, I was home alone with my mother when I heard someone call my name. There was no mistaking it. I heard it loud and clear. Since my mom was in the bathroom, I thought she was the one who had called me. It was possible she needed some toilet paper and wanted me to get it for her. So, I grabbed some and knocked on the door to hand it to her. Now that I am a mother, I have come to understand that bathrooms are often one of the only places where mothers can find some solitude in their endlessly busy lives, so you can imagine how pissed she was when she responded with;

"What do you want? I'm using the restroom."

At that moment, I was confused.

"Here is the toilet paper. Why did you call me? I thought you needed toilet paper."

"I didn't call you!" she snapped back.

Obviously, she hadn't called me. So, I returned to the living room, a little shaken.

Then I heard my name again.

At this point, I thought my mother was teasing me, so I ran back to the bathroom and said,

"Mom, I know you called me. I heard you again."

She initially responded by saying she didn't call me, but when I lingered, not knowing what to do, she concluded with, "Danelle... It's probably your father. Next time you hear your name, respond."

At the time, it had been a long while since my dad had interacted with me, so all the things that I had been taught by the church started to resurface.

"Mom, I'm scared!" I said.

She calmly responded, "Danelle, if you are afraid, tell your father. Tell him you are scared, and you don't want him to come to you anymore."

I did just that and never heard from him again. Since then, there have been moments when I was down in the dumps and would have given my last breath just to hear my father or feel his presence one more time. Even those desires made me feel ashamed because I still believed it was wrong and demonic.

I have dreamed about how different my life would have been if my father had not died. I resented the church for making a little girl believe that her dad's presence was demonic. I questioned God and His ways. Why did He take my father before I got a chance to make memories with him? Memories that I could call ours. I envied my cousins, friends, and other family members who had their fathers. Even though I had lost my father before I even knew how it felt to have one, it didn't make me miss him any less.

I often fantasized about the future; I would have a loving husband, a strong family, and a happy home. My husband would shower me with all the affection I needed and protect me from ever getting hurt again. I wouldn't make the same mistakes my mother made. I would grow up to become the perfect wife, and I would have a perfect life. Most importantly, I would never be alone or vulnerable enough to be taken advantage of again.

My father's spirit and conflicting teachings had confused me. I felt ashamed for thinking that it was the love my father had that wouldn't let him leave us and made him stay around to protect us. I might have felt ashamed, but I couldn't help but wish he was around anyways. There was a time I wished that more people, other than myself, had encounters with my father's spirit so I wouldn't feel crazy or judged. I prayed to be able to share the experience with someone, anyone! But was it demonic or was it just my father? Who was talking to me?

Chapter 3

If You Tell, You'll Regret It

When a child grows up without a father, many things are unnoticeably different for them. Fathers are meant to protect, provide, and give structure to their families. In their absence, their wives and children are left vulnerable and defenseless to many things.

My mother did the best she could despite her predicament. After my father passed, she kept on working and showered my brother and me with gifts and attention. During this period, she also dated a couple of men but ended up settling with none of them. My brother and I loved one of the guys she met though. He was so nice to us that he stole our hearts. To make things better, he even played with us whenever he could. With him, we felt loved and accepted and we saw our mother smile again. When they were together, things were perfect, and we were happy. However, they never agreed to be in a committed relationship. When I was about six years old, my mom met a new man. They began dating, but I felt he wasn't into us as much as the previous guy. My brother felt the same way, and we both wanted her to pick the first guy. But she chose the one we felt wasn't as bonded to us as we so badly desired.

Shortly after they began dating, my mother started acting differently. She would spend hours in the bathroom, and by the time she was out, the stench of foul-smelling smoke would overcome it. At the time, we thought our mother was smoking weed, and we believed that the weed was to blame for her weird behavior. So, my brother and I came up with a plan to eliminate it. We chose a day when she wasn't home; we took her bag of weed and threw it into the street. Then we reasoned that she would find the weed or someone else would, and they would use it. So, we picked the weed off the streets, brought it back into the house, rubbed it in Vaseline, and then threw it back into the street. There, we resolved the issue for once and for all, we proudly thought. We were not liars and was proud of our intervention, so when our mother returned, we told her what we had done. We let her know that we didn't want her smoking because it negatively affected her. After listening to us, she apologized and promised never to smoke again.

It turned out we were naïve. We thought we had solved the problem and our old mother would return to us. We had no idea what addiction was. We also had no idea that the substance our mother was smoking in the bathroom was not weed. It was crack cocaine. Her new boyfriend had introduced her to crack, and she had gotten hooked. She thought she could just stop, but she couldn't. As far back as I can remember, that was the beginning of the downward spiral of my childhood. It felt like I was sliding down a razor blade into a bucket of rubbing alcohol. I already didn't have a father, and now I had lost my mother to drugs.

As my mother was changing, so were my friends' parents. Whenever we were at my paternal grandmother's house, we had a lot of friends in the neighborhood to play with. After the crack hit our community, it was all around us. Back then, my mom only had to walk around a corner to find guys who were more than ready to sell her the substance. It was called 'curb serving' in those times. The situation also placed us in the middle of rival gangs. So, it was clear that all of our homes were affected.

My father's mother raised chickens when I was very young. After she stopped raising chickens, she allowed us to turn the chicken coop into a clubhouse. This turned into the neighborhood get-away spot for all the kids in the neighborhood to escape from the changes we were experiencing at home. We lived across the street from a field, where everyone would dump unwanted things. It was like going shopping for us! We got curtains, paint, wood, old mattresses, even an old oven; everything we needed to make our clubhouse into a home. We built rooms and my grandmother even gave us old clean sheets to put on the beds. We'd use the old stove with wood to heat the clubhouse. We played in there nearly every day.

One of the kids that lived in the neighborhood that used to come over to play initially had both parents together in the home. When his mother got addicted to crack, it tore their marriage and home apart. We often saw his mother roaming the street. She had gotten so frail that she looked like she would drop dead any minute. Whenever my friend heard that we had seen his mother, he would burst into tears. He was ashamed of her and the fact that everyone knew they were related.

My life was not much different. My mother continued to work nights seasonally. That coupled with her addiction, she started leaving us with my dad's mother often. As I mentioned earlier, my dad's mother kept many men around that she serviced daily. I was a young and pretty girl in a home that sexually-driven men constantly occupied; it was far from an ideal environment. However, my mother knew that I would never be hungry, thrown out, unsupervised, or beaten under my grandmother's roof. She was naive to other possible dangers.

There was a particular man that frequented my grandmother's home. The community knew him as 'Willie B., The Booty Getter'. At the time, I was just six years old, and from my young perspective, he looked tall and his shoulder-length hair appeared to be jerry curled. He was also dark, loud, and constantly in overalls. My grandmother had a recliner right at the end of the hall, resting on the wall that separated the living room from the kitchen. So, to go out through the front door, you had to get past the recliner.

All the kids from my neighborhood came to our house to play in the clubhouse. Meanwhile, Willie B., The Booty Getter, who had gotten his foul name from his penchant for young girls, would strategically sit in the recliner by the door. Then, whenever the girls passed by him to get outside, he'd grab them and pretend to tickle them while he fondled their private parts.

All the while, I had been really good at not getting caught. Then one unfortunate afternoon, while I was avoiding him, he managed to grab me. I can remember how his strong arms suddenly grabbed my waist, lifting my feet off the ground. The next thing I knew, I was in his lap. I was wearing shorts and a t-shirt. Willie B. began to tickle me and, without hesitation, slid his hand up the leg of my shorts.

Immediately, I jumped down from his lap and went straight into the kitchen where my grandmother was cooking. I looked her straight in the face and told her what Willie B. had done to me. Her response shocked me. She called me a liar and told me to go outside to play. I was confused. I had expected him to get into trouble. I thought the adults in my life were supposed to protect me. So why would she automatically assume I was lying? Did I do something to make her feel I would lie about such a thing? I went outside embarrassed and sad.

Later that week, the ice cream man came through the neighborhood. All the kids were excited, screaming, "Ice cream, Ice cream! We want ice cream!" Willie B. was also around, so he stopped the ice cream man and asked all the kids what they wanted. I stood there, patiently waiting for him to ask me what I wanted. But after getting everyone else's order, he deliberately scanned around to make sure nobody was left out. I was the only one standing there without ice cream.

Then, he looked me dead in my face, in front of everyone, and said, "I'm not buying you an ice cream because you're a lying bitch."

I shrunk in embarrassment. Of course, none of my friends were going to give up their ice cream just because I didn't get one.

Soon, it became the norm to call me foul names in the house. I was called everything from fast to hot. I didn't know what those words meant at the time, but within me, because I enjoyed the attention and being loved, I felt they were telling the truth. Those words were thrown at me so often that I didn't realize I was still a virgin. Nobody ever told me what virginity was, and since I was molested and fondled throughout my childhood by different men, I thought I had lost my virginity when I had never actually had sex. So, when people would try to humiliate me and belittle me by asking me if I was a virgin, I'd shamefully say, "No."

    I craved attention. I was timid until I found the stage. I started dancing at a young age, and I dreamed of becoming a dancer for MC Hammer. My mom would pay my brother and me to dance for her and her friends while she was entertaining them. In those moments, I would let loose. I remember listening to Janet Jackson and doing dances like the snake and centipede. I even participated in the community center talent shows and thoroughly enjoyed them. Those times made me feel seen. I knew people enjoyed seeing me dance. They paid attention to me and complimented me. These were some of the rare moments when I felt confident.

Chapter 4

You Just Don't Belong, Little Momma

When I was seven, my mom got pregnant. My brother and I were beyond excited. The idea of having a baby sibling filled us with so much joy. However, our mother was in rehab during her pregnancy, so we were forced to live with her parents, our grandparents. My grandmother hadn't changed. She was still very strict. Her house was also never empty, and there was never a time when we could say we were alone. In other words, privacy was nonexistent. My mother had five siblings growing up; a brother and four sisters. They were a close-knit family, so my cousins were always around, and we were all raised like siblings.

My grandmother would harshly discipline us for what seemed like the smallest things. She whipped us even when we hadn't done anything wrong, and we even got whipped when we played like normal kids. Every time she returned from work, there was always a reason for a whipping either with a switch or a belt and most of the time, we didn't deserve it. My grandfather, on the other hand, could not stand any of it. Immediately, my grandma started with the whipping, he would go into his room and return only after she was done to console us in any way he could. There was one time when grandma whipped us so hard and for so long that I remember seeing him get up from the chair he had been resting on, shaking his head while holding back tears. I remember watching him wipe a tear from his eye. It was just too much for him. Through all of this, my brother and I couldn't wait for our mom to get out of rehab so we could just move back into our own home.

When our mother got out of rehab, we got everything we wanted at the time; we moved back into our home, and our mother gave birth to a baby boy. My older brother and I spoiled him like he was ours. He was eight years younger than me, and his father returned to prison while he was still a baby. Our neighborhood hadn't changed since we left, so my mother relapsed and started using drugs again not too long after our return. As the oldest girl, I took on most of the responsibility of watching and taking care of my baby brother.

One day, while I was home from playing with a friend who lived down the street from me, something terrifying happened. At the time, my baby brother was in the same room with us, and I thought my mom was in the kitchen or living room. Suddenly, the fire alarm went off. I called for my mom, but there was no answer. In school, we learned about fire outbreaks and what to do in the event of one. We were afraid that the house was on fire. There were bars on the windows, and the only way out was through the front door. So, I touched the doorknob to see if it was warm, but it was cool. I grabbed my baby brother, placed a light blanket over his head, and cradled him in my arms as we got down on our knees to crawl out of the room. By the time we opened our room door, the house had been engulfed by smoke. Once again, we stuck to the routine and held our breath as we crawled and finally reached the front door. It was only when we got to the front door that we finally stood up. We began walking down the street towards my friend's house, hoping to see my mom on the way. Thankfully, we did. She was coming from around a corner when she spotted us. She was shocked to see us outside on the streets with my little brother at night, so she asked us why we were outside and what we were up to. I simply told her that the house was on fire. She immediately ran to the house and found the source of the smoke. A pot of rice on the stove that she was cooking had run out of water and started to burn. Luckily, nothing in the kitchen nor the house had caught fire. But my mom was impressed with me, and she praised me for taking control of the situation. At that moment, I remember feeling proud of myself for knowing what to do.

However, our problems were far from over. As usual, due to my mom's drug use, she would get behind on the mortgage, and to avoid losing the house, she would have to rent it out and be forced to move in with either her parents or my dad's mother. My father's mother lived on the West side of town, where the predominantly poor minority families lived. On the other hand, my mother's parents were more financially well off and lived on the north side of town which was occupied mostly by wealthy white families. So, when we were staying with my mom's parents, we were transferred to the white school that had only six other black students attending. We were transferred to the low-income public school at my dad's mother's, where the teachers didn't even want to come to school. This time, my mother decided to stay with my dad's mother. As I got older, I became insecure, timid, and fearful. I craved acceptance. But I didn't feel any safer in school, around girls my age, than I did around the molesters.

There was a large family that lived around the corner from my grandma's house; they had a lot of female relatives. Some would say they were ghetto; I would agree. They hated me for some reason that I couldn't figure out. I hadn't done anything to offend them, but they would bully me whenever they saw me around the neighborhood. One day, on my way home from getting frozen slushies at a candy house, I ran into them. They hated me like they were getting paid for it. When they approached me, they began saying that I thought I was better than them because my hair was longer. One of them even threatened to slap my slushy out of my hand. I was so terrified that I was fine with the slushy being slapped out of my hand as long as she didn't hit me. Unsurprisingly, before I could say a word, they went for my slushy, and I walked away without defending myself while they laughed.

But the bullying didn't stop, and my bullies did not give me a chance to catch a break! Every day, they would punk me in front of the school, and I lived in constant fear of being beaten up. I knew if I told my mother, she would make me fight and I was too scared to fight, so I hid. An empty field separated our elementary school from the residential neighborhood we all lived in, and we had to cross that field every day to get to school. So, in the 6th grade, I would leave the house like I was going to school, but instead, I would stop at the field and sit there all day until school was over. No lunch, no protection, just sitting there in the field alone, hoping no stray dogs, snakes, or rats would come my way. Above all, hoping I wouldn't encounter the bullies. Sadly, despite the danger of being in the field, I felt much safer there than at school.

When my bullies hadn't seen me at school for about a week, they decided to show up at my house. Three of the girls from the family that hated me knocked on my door and told my mom to bring me outside because they wanted to fight me. Staying true to her combative nature, my mom obliged. I stood face to face with one of the girls while my mom stood in the middle. As the neighborhood kids began to gather around the yard to watch the fight, I was shaking inside. At some point, everything froze. It was like I had an out-of-body experience, and was staring down at myself. All the while, it was difficult for me to believe it was actually happening. An entire week of skipping school and waiting out in the fields was not enough to keep these girls away?

"Hit her, Danelle! Punch her in the face!"

I heard my mother scream these words to me suddenly. She was serious about this fight even though it was clear that I would do anything to avoid conflict.

I looked at my mom and said, "I don't want to fight."

I thought she would defend me, and the girls would be afraid to mess with me again, or at the very least, they would go home. But I was wrong. My plea fell on deaf ears.

My mom repeated her instructions without missing a beat, "Hit her, Danelle! I'm standing right here. What do you think I'm going to let her do to you? Don't let her hit you first!"

But I had a different strategy. I believed that if I didn't hit her, then she wouldn't hit me. There would be no reason, and it would be a non-violent stalemate. No punches would be thrown. I couldn't have been more wrong. The girl punched me so hard that I busted my lip.

After getting hit, I got mad enough to fight, but my mom was already disappointed.

She pushed me into the house while yelling, "Get in the house! I told you not to let her hit you first!" I felt humiliated, and hot tears streamed down my face.

As my mother pushed me into the house, some of the girls yelled out, "And you bet not come to school tomorrow, or we gon' beat you up again."

My mother stopped and replied, "Oh, she'll be there!"

I was beyond terrified! I prayed that if the dear Lord loved me, He would take me in my sleep, and I wouldn't have to face the next day. Unfortunately, He didn't take me. The next morning, my mother woke me up early and sat me down in my grandmother's living room, where she wrapped each of my fingers with toilet paper to protect them from the twin beads that she then tied around each knuckle. The twin beads were hair accessories with big round knockers on their end, and they all sat perfectly on top of each knuckle. My mother told me to keep my hands in my pocket and when the girls approached me at school, to pull my fist out and punch one of them dead in the mouth. She said when the other girls see the blood squirting out of her mouth, they will back off.

Again, I was too terrified for something that violent. I wasn't sure if I had it in me. All I knew was that something had to be done.

My mother and older brother walked me to school that day. As soon as we got on campus, my mother tried escorting me to the classroom, where she thought I would have protection with the teacher. But the teacher in the classroom refused to open the door. Eventually, the girls saw me on campus, gathered all the kids around, and came up to fight me. There were five girls in total, all standing in my face, trying to provoke me to fight. While this was still on, a male cousin of theirs ran up behind me and slapped me hard in the back of the head. He tried to run away, but my mother caught up with him quickly and slapped him in the back of his head so hard, that he went sliding across the dusty blacktop.

As he got up from the ground with dust covering one side of his body, head, and face, he angrily approached my mom, planning to retaliate. Thankfully, my brother swiftly intercepted him and stood in front of my mother, as if to say, "you will have to go through me, mister" Now, this cousin of theirs knew well to pick his fights and to confront my brother wasn't on his list, so he ran home crying. As all the kids began marching around the playground fence, chanting, "We hate Danelle!" the principal who had gone to high school with my parents came running out of the office screaming, "Katrena, Katrena! You can't be hitting these kids!".

My mother replied, "The hell I can't when they're hitting my daughter, and your teachers won't open the classroom door or come out to help!"

That day, I was withdrawn from the school, and to protect me, my mother immediately transferred us back to the white school in her mother's neighborhood. Finally, the bullying was behind me. The new school had so much more to offer than my last school, and the teachers seemed happy to be there. I was beginning to feel like I could finally fit in. However, not too long after transferring, I began to notice that I was treated differently by the teacher and students. The kids freely made black, slave jokes to me in front of others, I was always picked last for teams, and of course, I didn't expect any of the boys to find me cute. I once again found myself in a situation where I wasn't good enough to fit in and where I was constantly being teased and bullied. The only difference was that I didn't have to fear getting beat up.

My mom's boyfriend got out of prison for a short time, and during the time he was out, my mom got pregnant again. My mother didn't want to have another baby that quickly, and she wasn't even attempting to get clean again. But her man was out and they were partying freely together. My mother went into labor when she was just seven months pregnant and gave birth to a girl that weighed just 2 lbs 2oz. I was nine years old at the time, and I finally had a sister. Mom stayed in the NICU for months, and since children weren't allowed within the NICU, I had to wait before I could see and hold my baby sister.

By the time she was released, she weighed only 4 lbs. She was so tiny she could fit inside my shoebox. My mother had had to have an emergency C-section to deliver my sister, so we moved back in with her parents so that she'd have the necessary support. One morning while I was getting ready for school, I heard my mom and her boyfriend in the next room arguing because neither of them wanted to be responsible for the baby. I heard the topic of adoption come up and it shook me to my core. I couldn't stand the idea of giving my baby sister away. She had just come home. So, I intervened. I begged them not to give her away. I promised them that I would take care of her by myself if they let her stay. They would hardly have to do anything. To my surprise, they agreed to my proposal. I was told that they would keep her while I was at school, but the moment I returned, she was my responsibility.

My sister was a preemie, so she had special needs as an infant. For one, she had to be fed every two hours. This meant that I would have to set my alarm clock in intervals and wake up every time it went off to feed her. Sometimes, I wouldn't even sleep. I'd stay awake and keep myself up by watching Winnie The Pooh while trying to lull my baby sister back to sleep. Coupled with this impossible sleeping schedule for a 9-year-old, I also had to be up and ready for school in time. I had to stay on top of my homework and grades. My mom resumed her night shifts, so I had to come straight home from school to take care of my little brother and sister. I had to ensure that they didn't get on my grandmother's nerves, and I also had to feed them, bathe them, keep them out of trouble, and put them to bed. My mother would get home between 1 a.m. and 2 a.m., and if my chores weren't done, she would wake me and tell me to do them. Other times, it wasn't my mother's voice that would wake me up. I loved my little brother and sister, and I saw them as my own kids. In my mind, I felt like everything was preparing me for the family that I had fantasized about having. I missed being able to play with my friends like the other kids, but they didn't really like me anyway. At least, I had my little brother and sister that needed me. I was determined to protect them from the things I wasn't protected from.

Despite the drug abuse and his back-and-forth vacations to the Big House, my mom and her boyfriend continued to stay together for years. Even though he had many flaws I appreciated never having to fear that he'd touch me inappropriately, nor did he beat my mother or cheat on her. We moved back into the house that my parents had purchased, and my brother, who had never been in any serious trouble, had gotten into enough fights to build a reputation not many in our neighborhood were prepared to test. There was one kid that used to come to play with him. My mom and I didn't like him. We felt that he was taking advantage of my brother, but my brother defended him. He made excuses for him and tolerated him. Our elementary school sold ice cream after school. One day my mother gave us money to get ice cream. It was a 50/50 bar, and I couldn't have been happier when I got mine. After getting the ice cream, my brother, his friend, and I headed home together. As we walked towards the school's exit, my brother's friend started making fun of me, deliberately knocked the ice cream out of my hand, and started laughing.

    My brother had not responded to all the other things that we felt crossed the line, but he was way off when he put his hands on me. My brother punched him in the face, and he fell to the ground. Then, my brother continued beating him while saying, "You don't touch my sister!" I was shocked! But within me, I was proud of him. I had never felt so protected. That was my brother! In my mind, he filled the shoes of my father. I saw him as my protector, companion, and confidant. Above all, he gave me unconditional love and I felt safe.

Chapter 5

SEEN BUT NOT SEEN

Our mother had changed and our lives had also changed. As my brother and I struggled to adjust to our new life, we also struggled to adjust to our new mom. Some of our family members even started treating us differently. It was like they didn't trust us because our mom was on drugs. There were times when our bags would be checked before we were allowed to leave their home after babysitting us. Our own family didn't trust us. My brother was smart, but he began to struggle with his studies in school. So, my mom promised him that if he got straight As on his report card, she'd buy him a Kawasaki dirt bike. Fortunately, the incentive worked. He got all As, and my mom took us to the Kawasaki dealership and allowed him to pick out a dirt bike. He was so happy when he got it. We lived across the street from the fields, so he would go into the fields and ride it all the time. Our father's mother stayed across the fields and my mother would allow my brother to ride back and forth from their place.

One day, we came home from school to find that his dirt bike was not in the garage. We searched everywhere for his bike, but we couldn't find it. At some point, I began to feel my brother's pain. Eventually, our mother told us that her boyfriend had stolen the bike and sold it to buy drugs. We thought we could just find it and get it back, but my mother said she had no idea where to find him or the bike and that she would try to replace it one day. My brother was livid, and that event only intensified the hate we both felt for her boyfriend.

There were good memories from my childhood as well. Every year, my grandparents would take all their kids and grandkids to the mountains, and we would rent a cabin on the lake. We'd play games, fish, swim, rent boats, and enjoy quality family time. These moments were the best experiences of my childhood. After completing the 6th grade, I was looking forward to starting Junior High School. I had made a friend from elementary school who was one of the only other black girls at our school, and her name was Jolene. She lived just a few blocks away from us and we hung out together at each other's houses. She had lots of cool stuff in her home, including a pool. She also had a brother that would come to hang out with us all the time. His name was Landon.

Landon and I grew a liking for each other. For the most part, he was a gentleman. To his credit, most boys his age were immature to some degree. The reason I really liked him was that he didn't push me to do things that I wasn't ready to do. Whenever I said "no" to him, it didn't affect the interest he already showed toward me. He spent a lot of time with me even though he lived across town. Friends of ours would gather at Jolene's house, my house, or Landon's house, but we were always together. We had formed our little crew. My family really liked Landon too. However, I was still shocked when they invited him to join us on our summer family vacation.

My mom allowed him to take me on my first date, and unsurprisingly, she also allowed me to go on a double date with my cousin. So, Landon brought one of his friends, and they took us to the drive-in. We dated for about a year before Landon started expressing interest in having sex. I was only 13, and although I was afraid, I confided in my mother. She told me that he was three years older than me and going through puberty as a freshman in high school. She also told me that sex was physical, and if he decided that he wanted to do it with other girls, it didn't mean he didn't love me. She told me not to feel pressured and that I shouldn't stop him from being with other girls. We had to keep our relationship separate.

When I told Landon this, he took full advantage of that freedom. We were still best friends, so he would tell me everything he experimented with. He would always play "You Can Have A Piece Of My Love" by Guy whenever he was going to tell me he had been with another girl. By the time I entered my sophomore year of high school, a friend of my aunt had moved into my grandparent's house with us. She was a mother with three daughters, and one of the daughters was a year older than me. Her name was Crystal. Crystal and I bonded almost immediately and I began to look up to her as my big sister.

One day, Jolene told me she had something to tell me. She told me that she had invited Crystal over to hang out with her while she was babysitting for her aunt. Later that evening, she said that Crystal had also invited another male friend over to hang out with them. She went on to tell me how she felt Crystal was forward with the guy and ended up having sex with him. She went into detail about how Crystal was on her period and how it ended up being a big deal to the guy who wasn't aware.

As I listened, I remembered Landon telling me about a girl he had been with recently who was on her cycle and hadn't told him. He told me how he panicked when he saw all the blood. It didn't take me long to put two and two together, and without asking, I just knew she was talking about Landon.

So, I asked her flat out, "Was the guy Landon?"

She looked me dead in the face and said, "Yes, I'm sorry. I told them that if they didn't tell you, I would."

I was shattered. I loved him and although I knew he had been with other girls, I didn't think he'd sleep with someone close to me. I felt so betrayed by Crystal. We did everything together. We lived in the same house, shared the same clothes, and slept in the same bed. She was my sister. My big sister! How could she have done that to me, knowing how much I loved Landon? Why?

I wept my eyes out that day. Then I confronted them, and they both apologized, but it wasn't enough for me. I was still seething with rage, and I wanted to get even. I had not had sex yet because I'd thought my first time would be with Landon. Not anymore. As far as feelings went with Crystal, I was more than prepared to show her that I could play those tricks too.

Crystal was promiscuous. She brought grown men into our house and into the bedroom with her. What I found strange was my mother's reaction, or better still, her lack of one. She didn't appear to have a problem with Crystal's promiscuity. I would eventually find out that her mother was selling her daughter's body to men for drugs. However, I couldn't have cared at the time. I just wanted to hurt Crystal and I was determined to get back at her for the betrayal. So one day, I asked her a question with a motive. I made her think I'd forgiven her so she'd let her guard down.

I asked her, "Out of all the guys you see, which one do you love the most?"

She proudly told me, "Dontez."

I took note.

Dontez was a frequent visitor to our home. He was cute and always had lots of money handy. Every time he came around, he would flirt with me, but I ignored him on every occasion for two reasons; 1) I felt like he was Crystal's boyfriend, and 2) he was a grown man. But since he was the guy that Crystal loved the most, he was the one I had to have.

One day, while he was at the house visiting Crystal, he started flirting with me as usual. Without knowing at all what I was getting myself into, I turned to look him dead in his eyes and just smiled. I didn't have to say a word; that was it. As I turned back around to walk away, he hastily pursued me. He gave me his pager number and told me to use the code 02, and he would know it was me and call me right back. I felt offended by the gesture because I thought that meant there was another girl that was #1. I told him sternly that I was either the only one or nothing at all. I could not come second to or stand beside anyone. He said he liked my spunk, and I naively thought I had shown how mature and strong I was. However, he was mature enough to know that he was dealing with a child's mind, so he quickly came up with a satisfying response.

He said, "No, baby girl, you're special. 02 means second to none." He flipped it so seamlessly that I took the bait just as he planned.

Dontez wasn't very tall, but he had a sun-kissed fair complexion, a perfectly lined up goatee, was very muscular, and wore his hair in a nice fade with deep waves. He drove a white Mustang 5.0, and on the side of the car, in chrome, his name was inscribed. Although I didn't know him, I came to learn how popular he was with the ladies in town. He had no shame in showing interest in me when Crystal was around. The same evening I gave him my number, he called the house. 'Perfect!' I thought. Crystal answered the call with excitement. I thought he would play it off and talk to her like he never got my number, but I was impressed when he quickly told her to put me on the phone. She was shocked as she handed the phone to me and walked away.

As I began talking to Dontez, I was really clueless about what I was getting myself into. I was just a young girl trying to get even with a friend that had hurt me. Dontez cleaned the offices of the doctor in the area where I lived. One night, he called me while he was at the office cleaning. He asked if he could pick me up so we could hang out while he cleaned the office. I was nervous but didn't want to act like a kid, so I agreed. I snuck out of the house, and he picked me up from the residential corner down the street from my house. I was so nervous that I was going to get caught or someone would find out I was gone. I felt sick to my stomach but went against that gut feeling anyways.

I made sure to wear jeans and a sweater so that if he tried anything, it wouldn't be easy. To my surprise, I followed him around the office, and we just talked while he cleaned without even brushing up against me. At the end of the night, when he was dropping me back home, he asked me if I needed any money. I embarrassingly said no. He asked me if I had any money. Again, I said no. He laughed and said, "So why don't you need any?" I was not used to people being nice to me or giving me things. I didn't know how to accept anything. As I sat in the passenger seat of his car, I held my head down and softly said, "Well, I guess I could use just a little." He asked me how much money I wanted, and I told him 20 dollars, hoping I hadn't offended him by asking for too much. He laughed and handed me $20 from a wad of money he pulled out of his right-side pocket.

When I got home, I was terrified to go into the house. I just knew a beating would definitely be my punishment in addition to being humiliated with religious judgment and my entire family would be gossiping about what I'd done. Nevertheless, I crept along the side of the house that led to the backyard. I was staying in the room that had a door that led to the backyard so I was lucky. I crept very quietly through the door and noticed it was still dark, and nothing looked out of place. Everyone was still sleeping. I had gotten away with sneaking out for the first time in my life. I quickly threw my pajamas on and tried to get a little sleep before school the next day. But as I lay in bed, the only thing that filled my thoughts was Dontez. I couldn't stop thinking of him and how good it felt to be paid attention to, to be told I was special. I wasn't ready to end things.

I snuck out to the house a few more times, and the same things would happen. We'd talk, and when he dropped me off, he'd ask me if I needed any money. I always only asked for $20 since it was the same amount he had given me the last time. I knew he would give me that amount and I didn't want to push my luck. The fourth time I snuck out, he asked me again if I needed any money as he was dropping me off. I responded with the same, "I could use $20." He smiled, stared at me a little, and handed me some folded-up money. Then he rubbed the back of his hand gently across my face. Then, he leaned in and kissed me. It felt good. I smiled from ear to ear.

He looked at me and said, "You have the most beautiful smile. I can't believe you are so young. You're mine. You are going to look back one day when you're grown, and I will still be here. I'm going to be your loudest cheerleader at your graduation. You are beyond beautiful."

Wow! I had never heard so many compliments at once. I went home as usual. Once I got into the house and began to get undressed, I pulled the money he had given me out of my pocket. As I unfolded the money and counted it, I discovered that he had given me $300. That was more money than I had ever had. I called him immediately to thank him. He told me that I deserved it and I needed to go shopping in the mall the next day. I did. Before then, I had never shopped at the mall before.

At school, I felt better. I did not need the money but I could at least buy myself lunch instead of depending on what the school provided. However, there was a time when I really needed money. During biology class, we were required to pay lab fees, and I did not have the amount they were asking for. I had also spent all the money Dontez had given me, so when I got home, I asked my mother for it, but she said she didn't have it. I was a good student and I didn't want to be in a situation where I wouldn't have the money to pay the lab fees. It would be too embarrassing for me to bear. Later that night, as I talked to Dontez on the phone, I vented to him about my situation. I didn't ask him for help nor did I expect him to fix things for me. The next day, I went to school, and before lunch, I got a call to come to the office, which was very unusual as my mother didn't have a car, and the only time she came to my school was when there was a problem or family emergency. When I got to the office, I was stunned to see my knight in shining armor, decked in an all-white sweatsuit, Dontez.

He handed me a handful of money, grabbed me and hugged me tightly. He even walked me off campus with his arm around me. The lunch bell had just rung, so everyone was coming out of class. I felt so proud to be walking around with him. Everyone was looking and I didn't care that he was way older than me. I also didn't care that he wasn't a student because none of the students had given me the kind of attention Dontez was giving me. It also didn't help that R-Kelly and Aaliyah were big at the time, and *'Age Ain't Nothing But A Number'* was everyone's favorite. I thought to myself how something that started as just a plan to get even with my friend could have led me to genuine love. I felt lucky. Was it possible that Dontez truly loved me and we'd be together forever?

That night when I snuck out of the house to go hang with him at the office, I was putty in his hands. I was so into him; it was obvious. As we entered one of the patients' rooms, we locked eyes and began kissing passionately. He pressed forward as I took slow steps backward. His hands had started to roam my body, grabbing my butt and my breast, then pulling the back of my hair and kissing my neck. The sensation was overwhelming. I was tingling in parts of my body I had never felt energy before.

I took one more step back, and he picked me up and laid me back on a stretcher. Then, he began to pull my pants off. I didn't stop him. I was nervous, but I thought I was finally ready. I thought he would just pull his pants down, and we would "do it." Instead, as I lay on my back, I felt his warm breath between my legs. I thought maybe he was going to kiss my leg and then move up. He stayed down there. Suddenly, I felt a sensation that I had never felt before. He was licking me down there. Oh my gosh! All I could think about was the fact that I hadn't taken a shower since the morning before school and I pee from there. I hoped he wouldn't get grossed out or ask me to do him too because I would be grossed out.

The feeling of him licking me felt good, but I was so insecure I wanted him to stop. As he made his way up, I prepared myself. He slid his pants down as he kissed my belly. He then climbed on top of me and inserted his penis inside of me. It hurt! I thought it would start to feel good any minute like everyone says it does, but that wasn't the case. The further he put it in, the more it burned. I didn't want him to get angry at me, so I tried to keep going. In a way, I felt obligated to have sex with him. I also didn't want him to think I was teasing him. He went very slowly, but the pain got unbearable. I couldn't take it anymore, and I had to ask him to stop. He stopped immediately. I was afraid he would be upset, but he just kept kissing me. Shortly after, I got dressed, and he took me home. All the way home, he held my hand.

When I got home that night, I lay in bed thinking about what I had just done. As far as getting even with Crystal, I had accomplished that. Dontez didn't speak to her anymore, and she was hurt. Landon and I had broken up, but we kept in touch.

'Now what? Do I continue seeing Dontez?' I thought about all the money he had given me, how he had surprised me at my school, how he had not pushed me for sex all this time, and how he had stopped when it was too painful. I thought to myself, 'he must really love me.'

I thought about the boys my age and how they didn't have money or a car, so I wondered how they could even help me or spend time with me. My life was already complicated; I had two little siblings I was responsible for and a mother on drugs. So, I thought we would have better chances to get what we needed if I went with Dontez, regardless of his age.

We continued seeing each other occasionally and we tried sex from time to time. Each time, we would get a little further than the last. One night I paged him, and I got a call back from a woman. When I asked for Dontez, she blatantly told me that he was busy at the moment because they were both having sex. I heard him laugh in the background, and then she hung up the call. I was shocked. I thought he loved me. I cried and thought I would never speak to him again.

The next day, Dontez called me. I thought I was big, bad, and would give him a good piece of my mind. As I told him how upset I was, he just laughed and took everything lightly. He ended up telling me that it meant nothing and she was just a friend playing a joke on me. He told me I was his girl, and nobody could change that. I believed him initially, but when the 'jokes' kept recurring, I decided to pull away from Dontez and stopped paging and calling him. From that moment on, I made a firm decision to focus on school and go back to being a kid.

Chapter 6

WHO SAID WOMEN DON'T SEXUALLY ABUSE CHILDREN?

To look back at a time before Dontez, but after I met Landon, I remember we moved from my mom's parent's home back into the house my parents bought. Between the moving and Landon exploring his freedom, naturally, there were gaps of time when Landon and I would be distant and not see each other as often as we used to. During these times I would talk to other boys, but I was not sexually active. When I was about 14 years old, after we'd moved back into the house, while my mom was still addicted to crack cocaine, she continued to work shifts at night. The family across the street from us had lived there since before my parents bought the home and my mom got to know the family well. So, my mom felt comfortable with them around us. She decided to hire one of the young adult female relatives, who had a baby, to babysit my siblings and me when she went to work. Her name was Alicia.

Alicia was bi-sexual and tomboyish. She was tall, dark-skinned, had short hair, and had a thick figure. She was nice and it was a lot better than being home alone with my younger siblings all night. At this time, I was in the 8th grade, and as usual, I was being bullied. This time I was being bullied by a big girl named Tricia. Tricia was about a foot taller than me and was the star player on the girls' basketball team. She was built and carried herself like one of the guys. I had no idea why she decided to pick on me outside of the fact that I was smaller, timid, and easy prey. Since we'd moved back into our home, I had to catch the city bus across town to get to school, like so many others. Unfortunately, Tricia lived close to me and would be on the same bus. This made it easy for her to torture me not only at school but all the way home too. One day after being humiliated all day by Tricia in school, she also spent the entire bus ride home punking me. It was common for the students to sit at the back of the bus, away from the driver's supervision. On this day, Tricia would call my name and when I turned around, she'd insult me and all of the observing kids would laugh. Someone even threw a piece of paper at me and even though it hit the back of my head, I just ignored it and kept looking forward.

I went home noticeably upset. Alicia asked what was wrong. As I narrated to her how I was bullied, I noticed how she was showing concern and asking questions. She asked me what Tricia looked like and where she got off the bus. I told her that Tricia got off the bus at the stop after mine. Alicia told me to stay on the bus past my stop and to get off at Tricia's the next day. I was terrified but agreed. The next day was no different. Tricia spent the entire day at school making fun of me and making me a laughingstock.

On the way home, she was also her usual self, teasing me and getting all the kids to laugh at me and make fun of me. As we approached my stop, my stomach started to flip-flop. As I thought about what Alicia told me to do, I feared staying on the bus and getting off at Tricia's stop. What if Alicia didn't show up? Despite my fear, we approached my stop and I made it up in my mind that it was worth the risk. I wanted the bullying to stop. I stayed on as the driver pulled up to my stop. Tricia noticed that I did not get off and suddenly started to get quiet. I noticed how she kept her eyes on me with a look of confusion on her face. As we approached the next stop, Tricia stood and walked to the back door and waited for it to open. I stood and walked to stand right behind her. As the bus slowed down, I desperately looked out the window and prayed that Alicia would be there. When the bus stopped, I saw her! She was there! She came with her little brother, who we called 'Pooh', who was about 10 years old at the time.

Tricia stepped off the bus and I followed her. She looked back at me as if to ask why, but said nothing. As Tricia exited the bus, Alicia immediately started to confront her.

She said, "Are you Tricia? I hear that you have been messing with Danelle. Since you want to fight someone so bad, fight me!"

I stood in shock! The bus had gotten caught at the light so all of the students on the bus watched the entire encounter. Tricia responded timidly refusing to fight. She kept her head down and began to walk towards the corner where she was lucky enough to have a green light to cross the street in front of the bus. Alicia and her brother closely followed behind her provoking her to fight. Tricia tried to ignore them, the way I had tried ignoring her, but Alicia said, "I am over 18 so I won't fight you unless you are willing to fight me. But my brother is smaller than you. He is only 10. Fight him!"

Tricia said nothing. I was a little angry. How is it that she was so willing to fight me but was unwilling to fight a 10-year-old? As she continued ignoring Alicia and walking across the street, Pooh ran up behind her and kicked her in the back. Tricia stumbled trying to catch herself. This entire time, the kids on the bus had been watching and even opened the side windows allowing Tricia to hear them laughing at her. She never looked back. She kept her head down and kept walking.

I felt sorry for Tricia despite how mean she had been to me. I didn't want anyone to feel the way I felt. I just wanted her to leave me alone. However, I was still afraid that her bullying was not over. I still had to catch the bus with her and see her at school the next day. I was afraid that she would retaliate against me for what Alicia and her brother did to her.

Later that evening, I cried and pleaded with my mom to not make me go to school. I begged her to just move me to a different school. She would not budge. She told me to go to school and said if Tricia approached me, to pick up the heaviest thing I could lift and beat her with it. Just like before, I couldn't imagine myself doing anything violent, so I went to school just expecting a beating or at least more bullying.

The next morning as I got on the bus, I noticed that Tricia was sitting at the front. She didn't sit in the back with her normal crew. However, they were loud and rowdy as ever. Nobody said anything to me or about me but that didn't erase my fears of what would happen at school. As we got off the bus and crossed the street to our school's campus, I saw my mom's sister and her daughter approaching me. They were dressed in sweats and sneakers. They were living in my grandparent's home within walking distance from the school. My aunt told me that my mom had called her and asked her to come to the school because I was scared that a girl named Tricia was going to beat me up. They were protective and upset! They told me to point Tricia out. As I pointed at Tricia who was just walking onto campus, she made eye contact with me. My aunt and cousin headed straight for her and Tricia ran off-campus. I assumed she got on the bus and went back home because I didn't see her for the rest of the day. Tricia never spoke to me again.

Things were finally peaceful and I began to enjoy having Alicia around while my mom was working nights. One day, a couple of girls were caught kissing each other at school behind the baseball dugout. At this time, same-sex relationships were still very taboo and frowned upon. I went home and told Alicia what happened at school thinking she would say it was wrong or gross. Instead, she responded by saying, "What's wrong with that?" I was shocked by her response and didn't want to say I thought negatively about it because I didn't want to offend her. I believe that this conversation was the beginning of Alicia discussing same-sex attraction being acceptable to me. At first, Alicia was just nice to me, but shortly after this conversation, she began to show sexual interest in me. She would make comments about how pretty I was and would often stare at me and shake her head as if she was trying to fight back what she really wanted to say or do. It was clear that she was flirting with me. I tried to ignore her and play it off, but she didn't stop.

I had been going to church with my aunt and I enjoyed hanging out with the youth there. During our youth bible study, I met a boy named Jaylen that I thought was cute. He also acted as if he liked me. Like shy kids, we started passing notes and trying to sit by each other during class. Jaylen lived with both of his parents who were still married. His father was African-American and his mother was Caucasian. Jaylen was tall with loose curly black hair. He even had a mustache, although we were only about a year apart. Jaylen lived close to me and rode a small dirt bike. I liked Jaylen's personality. He was nice, kind, and never tried to touch me inappropriately, and we both enjoyed spending time talking about what we'd learned at bible class. I began to trust him and feel safe around him, so, I confided in him about Alicia.

Jaylen wanted me to tell but I explained my fear of what would happen if nobody believed me again, and what would happen to my little brother and sister if I left. He promised to keep my secret but felt like he had to do something to protect me. He came up with the idea that he would come over as much as he could and thought that if he was there, it would stop Alicia from trying to come on to me. He would drive his little dirt bike to my house and sit with me all evening after school. My mom liked him so she didn't have a problem with him coming over but we were told we had to sit outside together. So, Jaylen and I would just sit on the swing set in my backyard and talk. A couple of times my mom permitted him to take me on a short ride around the corner on his bike.

For a short while, the idea worked. However, when Alicia realized she would never get me alone, she began making up lies to my mother, saying that I had done things, or didn't do my chores so that my mom would say Jaylen couldn't come over. Unsurprisingly, when Jaylen wouldn't be allowed to visit, the touching and flirting continued. I grew terrified of her, but history had taught me that telling didn't mean I would be protected, so I kept it to myself.

One day, as I was standing at the sink, doing the dishes, Alicia came up behind me and put money in my back pocket. Then, she spun me around and stuck her tongue into my mouth. I was scared and disgusted. Her tongue tasted like mint gum and cigarettes. I wanted to throw up, cry, disappear, but all I could do was stand there in shock.

I wanted to leave, but when I thought of all the horrible things that could happen to my brother and sister if I left them behind with her, I could not find the will to go. I felt like it was my responsibility to protect them.

After a few months of being touched and kissed at the hands of my babysitter, I finally built up the courage to tell my mom. As I approached her early one Saturday morning, when I knew she didn't have to go to work that night, I decided to tell her. I silently hoped that she wouldn't respond as my grandma did, or worse, tell the babysitter what I said and leave her to watch me and my siblings. Since Alicia's family lived across the street, I feared that things would get worse if my mom told her what I accused her of. All I could think about is what happened to Tricia. But like with other things, I'd reached my breaking point. I couldn't take it anymore. Not only did I feel like I didn't fit in at school, I now hated to come home too. This early morning was the day. My mother was in the living room, sitting on the couch. I approached her and told her that I had something to tell her. She asked me what it was. I cautiously told her what the babysitter had been doing to me and how Jaylen was banned from the house only because she wanted to get me alone and that the reason he had been coming over so much was actually to try to keep me safe.

My mother was not pleased that I didn't tell her the first time it happened. I told her that I was afraid and that I was still afraid that after telling her the truth, Alicia or her family would retaliate. As a resolution, I asked for permission to go back to stay with her parents. However, I was still worried about caring for my younger siblings. My mother understood my fears and knew that she would not be home to keep me safe with the family across the street while she worked every night. So, she agreed to let me move back with her parents and assured me that she would take care of my little brother and sister, and she wouldn't let Alicia continue to watch them. Her response was all the assurance I needed, so I left.

At the time, my grandparents had experienced a fire in their home, so they moved to another house that they owned on the west side of the city while the former was undergoing repairs.

My grandfather was the funniest, most affectionate, and generous man I had ever been around. However, living with my grandparents meant that I had to follow their strict spiritual rules. It was mandatory to go to church. At first, I didn't understand why but when I saw the happy families in the church, I wanted what they had for the family I envisioned having. The lives of the families I saw became another goal for my future family. I tried very hard to put the abuse behind me, and I was grateful that reporting had improved my predicament for the very first time.

For years, we have known from research that high levels of father-child involvement are correlated with higher levels of confidence, self-control, and sociability. Consistent fatherly involvement has also been shown to reduce psychological problems and rates of depression in young women. It has become a joke to say a girl has daddy issues, but it is no laughing matter. If the child could do better, they would. They need love, understanding, and protection, not ridicule, and exposure to predators who will only see them as easy prey. They are doing their best with what they learned from their life experiences. When we hurt the vulnerable in our community, we can no longer blame others for our continued oppressed living, broken and divided society, and culture.

When I experienced these things, I dreamt more about what my life would be when I grew up. I thought having a husband would solve everything because I'd have love. I would no longer be an outcast trying to fit in, and he wouldn't let me get hurt by others. I could be me, and he'd see what everyone else couldn't see, and they would eventually regret how they treated me. Finally, all my pain would pay off. God wouldn't allow me to endure all of this without a great reward. These thoughts got me excited. I daydreamed of a Disney fairytale marriage where I would live happily ever after. Who knew that wishing for happiness and safety in a relationship would deplete one's ability to feel whole and complete alone? Who knew that desire would lead me to sacrifice myself to please others in hopes that I'd earn genuine love and acceptance? Life was about to teach me how it treats those whose security, happiness, and peace were dependent on things outside of themselves.

The most valuable thing you can do is tend to your inner healing. It is your priority to protect your purpose, which means you must value yourself healthily. When we lead broken, hurt and empty lives, we constantly look to superficial things or validation from people to fill the void that we can't seem to satisfy. This is our intuitive way of reaching for the grounding and nurturing we do not allow ourselves. You can't offer what you don't see in yourself. You can't be a blessing to others if you cannot see your value and love yourself. God is bountiful, productive, and peaceful. Tend to your dark inner corners and watch every area of your life multiply.

It isn't fair to compare one person to another. Many things factor into how a person perceives, processes, and responds to experiences. Two people with similar experiences will react to it in different ways. Their chemical make-up is different. From learning this, I discovered why telling my story is so important. I knew many others could relate. I wanted them to find confidence in their story by reading mine.

Chapter 7

Finding A Way to Fit In

A heavy dark cloud of insecurity was still hovering over me, and I still wasn't popular with the boys my age. Landon and I still saw each other occasionally, but we never reconnected as a couple. Most of the boys I went to school with, especially those around us, were afraid of my brother. I couldn't catch any cute boy's attention at my school because I didn't own designer brand clothing and shoes like the other popular kids. These things were important at our school. The boys at my school wanted popular girls who were desired by the other boys so they could show them off. So, while everyone knew my brother, I was a 'nobody'. People hardly even knew my name; they just referred to me as 'DJ's sister'.

I was still unpopular by the time I clocked 15-years-old. I had just finished my first year of high school, and I had gotten out of my shell a little. I joined the flag team and enjoyed performing during halftime at the football games. Finally, I had a life away from staying home with my little brother and sister. Although I still wasn't popular, I ended my first year with memories that I will never forget. Our football team had been the best that year, and we beat our opponents with a wide margin of 17 to 0.

The next year, I was transferred to another high school by my mom's parents' home. We called their area the "white side of town." After the ordeal with the bisexual babysitter and moving into my grandparent's home, I was put right down the street from a girl my age that I grew up with at my family's church. Her name was Brenda. She had a dark chocolate complexion, a small frame, curvy hips, and a beautiful smile. She was 16 and had a baby. Her parents were supportive of her, but they didn't like her baby's father and were strongly against the idea of her spending time with him. However, Brenda continued to see him secretly. At the time, she was also receiving government assistance, which made it possible for her to shop for her clothes while still having enough money to spare. She carried herself with confidence and had many admirers. We did not hang out outside of church until I began my sophomore year in high school.

Brenda's boyfriend lived right down the street from us. When she wanted to hang out with him, she would tell her parents that she was with me. I was the third wheel. Her baby daddy had a brother that I began to see around often when I was with Brenda, but we never really spoke to each other on a personal level. His name was Tyson. Tyson was cute to me, but he was a grown man. Brenda's parents owned multiple houses on the block. She was allowed to live in the home down the street from their main house, where they ran an elderly home. She worked there as the night keeper to help her make extra money to care for herself and her son. Her baby father's grandmother's house was next to that house, connected by one fence.

One day, while I was sitting in her front yard and Tyson was standing in his grandmother's yard, he spotted me. He came to the fence and started talking to me. It was a casual conversation. He spoke about how he had been noticing me but hesitated to talk to me because I was so young. I completely understood and felt the same about him. He was much older than me. However, I was attracted to him. Tyson had a very fair complexion and the most gorgeous green eyes. Tyson wasn't very tall. He was about 5'10 and had a stocky frame, but he was not fat. He also had sandy brown hair and wore it cut very low with natural waves.

The two brothers were popular in the neighborhood and were consequently pursued by many girls there. I enjoyed having a friend to hang out with, but I didn't enjoy being the third wheel whenever we spent time with Brenda's baby daddy. She began telling her baby daddy to invite his brother whenever we hung out. At first, Tyson and I didn't bond. I knew he was there to occupy my attention so his brother and Brenda could have some alone time. I didn't mind as I was doing the same. However, as we spent more and more time together, Tyson and I started liking each other, and we decided that we wanted to see each other outside of the time we spent with Brenda and his brother. So, we began seeing each other alone. Tyson was seven years older than me. After months of hanging out together, he began sneaking into my room at night after everyone had gone to sleep. He would hold me while I slept, and in my mind, I played house. I imagined that we were married and lying in our bed at night after a long day. I told him that I didn't want to have sex, and he agreed because he didn't want to get into trouble due to my age.

However, you can't play with fire and not expect to get burned. The more time we spent together, the more affectionate we became with one another. One night as we were cuddling, we started kissing. Things got heated, and we crossed the line.

Afterward, as we held each other, he said, "I'm upset with you." I was not expecting to hear those words after what we had just shared. So, I asked him what I had done to upset him.

He said, "You told me you wouldn't have sex with me. I expected you to stop us before we went that far."

I felt bad and ashamed. I apologized for not showing more discipline and felt like it was my responsibility to stop things.

He said, "I am just afraid because of your age, and I don't want to go to jail. I told myself that I would not let this happen, but I fell in love with you and couldn't stop myself."

I thought that meant we were in love, so he continued to sneak over at night. My mom used to be out late, so she usually wasn't home for the night. On one of those nights, we were lying in bed when we suddenly heard my mom come back home. Usually, whenever we hear someone awake in the house or come close to my room, he would leave. But since nobody usually came into the room, he thought it would be no different. So, this time he decided to jump into the closet to hide quickly, just in case.

My mom came straight to my room. I thought, 'okay, she will just ask me a question and keep going,' but she headed straight for the closet. 'Oh no. How did she know he was in there?' I was shaking like a leaf inside, hoping that Tyson would think to hide behind some clothes. As she pulled the handle to open the closet door, it opened slightly and slammed back shut. 'How stupid could he be!?' I screamed internally. He was holding the knob like it wouldn't be suspicious. Why didn't he hide? She pulled the knob again, but harder this time. The door swung open and immediately slammed back shut from the inside.

I sunk in my skin as my mother turned to me and said, "Danelle, who's in this closet?" I couldn't speak. I knew she'd kill me. She turned to the closet and announced, "If you don't come out, I will wake up my daddy and he has a pistol." The door creaked open. She scolded us both and made him leave. Then she left my room. 'That was it?! I didn't get hit? Wouldn't she tell my grandparents? God spared my life,' I thought.

Tyson was so scared that charges would be pressed against him that he began distancing himself. He had kids and was often seen around with his baby's mother. We fought about the other girls he saw, and eventually, we stopped talking. By this time, I knew I enjoyed the attention from having a boyfriend. I was still shy and didn't want to sleep around. I just wanted a boyfriend. However, having a boyfriend made me feel obligated to have sex with them to keep them. I started seeing a guy that was a little older than me but was still a teenager. His name was Jerome.

Jerome was known in town as well. He was cute and popular. Jerome was dark, thin, and had short hair. He still lived at home with his mother. My best friend knew him from around town. She had gotten tired of the issues between her and her baby's father, so she considered moving on. One night, we were supposed to go on a double date with Jerome and his friend, but her baby daddy called her at the last minute, and she decided to see him instead. So, she left me to go alone, thinking I'd be safe.

Jerome and his friend picked me up from Brenda's house, and we all went to his friend's house. They were about four years older than I was. None of their parents were at home at the time. They went into the kitchen to make drinks and came back with a dark blue plastic cup that had some liquor in it. Although I was trying to act grown and mature, I had not drunk before. They offered it to me, and because I didn't want to look immature, I accepted. Immediately I started drinking it like I was a pro, and shortly afterward, I started feeling weak. I felt like I could hardly hold my head up, so I asked my boyfriend if there was a place I could lay down for a minute. He escorted me to the bedroom down the hall to the left, the first door on the right. I laid down, and he said he'd come to check on me in a little bit.

When he left the room, I heard it lock from the outside. So, I stumbled towards the door and turned the knob, but it wouldn't open. At this point, the room was spinning, and I felt like I would pass out. I laid back down on the bed, fully clothed, and as I lay there watching the ceiling spin, I suddenly heard the door unlocking. My boyfriend entered the room and turned the lights off. He climbed onto the bed and laid next to me, and started rubbing my body. I started telling him to stop, but nothing was coming out of my mouth. It was like I was forming the words in my mind, but my mouth had timed out. Why couldn't I speak? Why did my body feel like a carload of bricks? I couldn't move, and I couldn't talk, but I was completely aware of what was happening.

He began pulling my pants and panties off. After getting them off, he climbed on top of me and began violating me. I lay there crying and staring at him with my eyes begging him to stop.

The television had been left on, and I could see his silhouette, but he never looked into my face. After he was done, he got up and left the room. Still unable to move, I lay there crying. A few seconds after he left the room, the door opened again. This time, it was his friend. He stood at the foot of the bed and pulled off his pants and underwear. I was still lying on my back, unclothed, unable to move. He immediately climbed on top of me and started violating me too. I fought and fought to try to move, but all I could manage to move were my fingers. With my fingertips, I reached for the part of his body that was within reach, which happened to be his arms that were stretched out on each side of me. I began scratching and digging my nails into him. He grabbed my hands and held them down to the bed and finished.

When the friend was done, he got up, put on his clothes, walked out of the room, and again, shut the door and locked it from outside. Even after everything I had just gone through, I was determined to not find myself just lying there. I was going to leave. So, I stumbled and held on to the wall and the bed, while I hurried to get dressed. A few minutes later, my boyfriend opened the door again to find me in tears, sitting at the foot of the bed. He told his friend that he needed to take me home.

It had already gotten late, and I was still unable to walk to the car, so they carried me. On the way to the car, I heard the friend tell my boyfriend that they should take me out to the country. Still unable to talk or defend myself, I sat in fear listening to their conversation, praying God would get me out of it. Finally, I heard my boyfriend say, "Naw. Just drop us off at my house, and she can stay the night." After they dropped me off, I lay in the bed next to him but didn't fall asleep. I was anxiously waiting for the morning to come so that I could catch the bus away from there.

By morning, I was up and out of there on the first bus. I caught the bus to my friend's house, where my mother thought I'd been all night. I told my best friend what had happened, and she encouraged me to report it, but history had proven how that could easily work against me. Moreover, I believed most people would not believe me. I'd be embarrassed and would have to tell my mother where I had gone, so I decided to keep it a secret. I was done dating. I had given up on boys or so I thought.

Fast forward a couple of years later, I saw on the news that Jerome's friend had been shot in the head while he was hanging out at a gas station in town. Then any years after that, I stopped by a store with my teenage daughter. I pulled up and parked next to a car with tinted windows. As I got out of the car to go inside the store, the driver's side window began to roll down. I heard someone call my name and when I turned, there was Jerome, my old boyfriend. He stretched his hand out of the window to shake mine. My daughter had joined me by the driver's side and quietly stood by, watching as I reached out to shake my abuser's hand. I never said a word. I let go of his hand and walked away. As my daughter and I walked away, she asked me who he was. I had already told her about the date rape so she got upset when she realized he was the one. She told me that I shouldn't have shaken his hand but I told her that I was healed and had forgiven him. While I felt free, he was the one who had to live with what he had done.

Girls with involved, loving, and respectful fathers have a template for how they should be treated. Their fathers are living, breathing, and active examples of how they ought to be treated by a man and therefore, they are less likely to become involved in violent or unhealthy relationships. Research has shown that children raised in fatherless homes are more likely to suffer from abuse and become abusers themselves. When the protector of the home is missing, the child is more likely to experience fear, and therefore, more fatherless children do not report abuse.

Chapter 8

So You Think You're Grown

Back when we were young, my brother had a girl he had been seeing since elementary school. So, naturally, he had also grown close to her brothers and family. I remember how I'd follow my brother everywhere he went, against his will, of course. However, he did not allow me to follow him too often when he'd hang out with the boys in the hood. He was too protective of exposing me to what was going on there. So, I would often be left home alone with my younger siblings. As my brother grew in his independence, I felt like I was in prison with no freedom or rights. My mom may have had an addiction, but she was very strict about many things.

With my father's passing, my mother made it clear to my brother that he was the man of the house and was responsible for protecting me. I remember having repeated nightmares about dead people. This fear came from believing that my dad's spirit would follow me, and it was not a good spirit, which made me fear all dead people. I would be afraid to sleep alone in my room. I would beg my brother to let me sleep in his bunk bed with him. He, on the other hand, enjoyed his privacy. He let me cry outside his door for almost an hour one day, begging him to let me in, but eventually, he opened the door. The fact that my mom had moved her boyfriend in was irrelevant, it's understandable why my brother didn't feel like he was the person to relinquish this role to. Naturally, there was a sort of a power struggle, expressed in frustration and at times, rebellion from my brother, to maintain his position and to continue to feel like he was the protector of the home. Because he felt like he had such a right to be an authority over me, it led to many arguments between him and me because I didn't accept him as an authority figure at the time. I felt like he was just a bossy big brother. Whenever he would tell me to do something, and I refused, he tried to force me to obey. This would lead to what I would call normal sibling rivalry disputes, and this was often! My brother and I were always at each other's throats, constantly fighting like cats and dogs over any small thing. My mom, on the other hand, got tired of playing referee to our disputes and hearing me constantly yell, "Mom!!! DJ….!!!" When I was about 13 years old and my brother was about 15 years old, we got into another one of our usual arguments. I don't even remember what we were fighting about. I am sure it was another stupid argument. Even though my brother was so protective of me that my mom couldn't discipline me without talking to him first, he felt like he had the right to discipline me without her permission.

On this day, we started arguing about something, and it continued from the bedroom to the hallway. He blocked me from going into the living room, and he started shoving me around and yelling at me. I, of course, started calling for my mom to make him stop him. Instead of my mom responding, her boyfriend, who was on parole, decided to intervene. He came to the hallway where my brother and I were and got between my brother and me and started pushing and challenging my brother to do to him what he was doing to me.

As he pushed my brother like he had been pushing me, he yelled, "Do something to me!"

My brother responded by telling him that he'd better get out of his face.

My mom's boyfriend responded with, "Or what?"

The incident escalated quickly. They began shoving each other back and forth and ended up in the living room where my mom's boyfriend showed his strength by grabbing my brother and holding him up against the wall, off his feet, and by his neck. I immediately felt defensive for my brother but thought it would stop soon. My brother has a very fair complexion, so when I started seeing him turn red, then a darker shade of red, I jumped on my mom's boyfriend's back and began yelling, "Let him go!" My mom then pulled me off and yelled at me about how her boyfriend was protecting me.

I assume my mom may have felt like her boyfriend would not go too much further and would let him go without hurting my brother. I didn't trust that. I felt like it had already gone too far. I thought quickly about him being on parole and ran for the phone and dialed 9-1-1. When the operator answered, my mom snatched the phone out of my hand and hung it up. They called right back, and by this time, my brother and her boyfriend were really going at it. He'd let my brother go and my brother went looking for the first thing he could find to hurt him with.

I had never seen my brother so furious. The dispute ended up in the front yard of our home with my brother chasing my mom's boyfriend around with a lead pipe or crowbar, I don't exactly remember. The police responded to the call and once they got into the situation, my mother was told that one of them had to go. It was decided. My mom felt like it was wrong to put her boyfriend out since it started with him trying to protect me, so my brother left that day.

My brother had not wanted to live with any of my family that would require him to go to church and not give him the freedom to hang out with his girlfriend and friends, so he ended up spending more and more time with his girlfriend and her family. Gangs were running rampant at this time and my brother and the people he hung out with had their crew too. He was focused on just trying to survive. Although he was still allowed to come home, he did not stay home often. He was not going to be treated as a child. He would come and go as he pleased. However, if I needed him, I knew how to reach him, and he would always come. Living my life with my brother not being around much as a protector made me more vulnerable, but I was not aware of how vulnerable I'd become.

One day, while I was riding the city bus, on my way home from school, I ran into a guy that looked familiar. When I was younger, while we were living in the home that my parents bought, my mom would often allow me and my brother to walk to the corner store.

I was about 12 years old, but I was physically developed and looked older. There was a store clerk that used to stare at me every time I went in. He was cute but I was young and not into boys, so I'd only look and keep going. I noticed that every time I left the store he would come outside and pretend to sweep the sidewalk and watch me walk all the way home. That was him on the bus. We made eye contact. He waved and smiled, and I returned the wave and smiled too. He got up from his seat and came to sit by me.

As we started talking, he told me that his name was Donnell. He went on to tell me that he had always had a crush on me and would watch me walk home when I left the store. I told him that I noticed. He told me that he was 23 years old. The same age that Dontez was. I told him I was only 15. We exchanged numbers anyway. Later that evening, we spent all night on the phone. He was different from Dontez. He didn't have money, but he was very into me.

He started catching the bus to my high school every day to walk me home and then get back on the bus to go home. I introduced him to my mom and family, and they actually liked him. I asked my mom why she didn't mind that he was much older than me. She said that I was mature for my age, and he was immature for his. My family allowed him to visit me regularly and even stay the night in the living room if he missed the last bus home.

My mom was still addicted to drugs and life at home wasn't getting any better. Donnell and I discussed how having a baby would be a way for me to be considered an adult so I would be able to move out. We agreed on the plan and the first time we had sex, we tried having a baby. After that day, we continued to discuss our plan but I wanted to go to college, and I became afraid that having a baby would hinder those opportunities. He agreed to support my dreams and we agreed not to try for a baby anymore.

I decided to get on birth control pills. I set an appointment at the local clinic because that way, I wouldn't have to tell my mom, get permission, or need an adult escort to be seen there. When I went to my appointment, they told me that they had to do an exam and pregnancy test before giving me birth control pills. I agreed. After the exam and pregnancy test, I waited in the room for the nurse to bring me my birth control pills.

The nurse entered the room and said, "We can't give you any birth control pills because you are pregnant."

I thought I was dreaming. All of a sudden, I felt like I was not in my body. I'd already changed my mind. I didn't want a baby anymore. I wanted to go to college. My grandparents are so spiritual. What will my family say? What will the church say? OH MY GOD!!! WHAT WILL MY MOMMA SAY?!!! I was so scared to tell my mother.

Later that day, I sat in my room at my grandmother's house just thinking about what I had gotten myself into when my older brother walked in. I knew if there was anyone I could tell, it was him, and he'd protect me from the backlash from my family. I told him I was pregnant and scared to tell our mother. Just like my big brother, he said he would talk to her first. He left the room and shortly afterward he came back and told me to go talk to her. I asked him what she said, and he said it was ok, and she wasn't that upset. He encouraged me again to go to the living room and talk to her.

I conceded. As I entered the living room, my mom was reclining quietly on the couch, watching television, like she had no clue what was going on. I sat on the couch across from her thinking, just in case she wanted to get violent, I would have a head start. I sat down and just looked at her. She asked me what was going on.

I said, "Well, DJ told you right?"

She responded with, "Told me what?" At that point, I knew she just wanted me to tell her.

I cowardly said, "That I'm pregnant," and I handed her the pregnancy confirmation from the clinic.

She opened the folded paper and looked at it.

She said, "Well, you better take that back and tell them they got it wrong because you are a virgin."

My shoulders slumped and my head fell to the left as I looked at her with an expression that begged for mercy. All I could muster up to say was, "Mom…"

She handed me the paper back and said "Okay."

Stunned, I said, "Okay?"

She repeated, "Okay."

Now I had to tell Donnell. I thought that although we had changed our minds, he would be happy to have a family with me. I called him on the phone to tell him the news. To my surprise, he was not happy.

He said, "Okay, so what are you going to do? I thought we decided it wasn't the best idea to have a baby. I think you should have an abortion."

I was hurt. I was raised to not believe in abortions and couldn't imagine taking our baby's life. I told him that he knew my beliefs and that I couldn't do that. He accepted my decision but his affection toward me changed. He began getting distant and treated me like I was disgusting.

I couldn't avoid it any longer; being that we were living with my grandparents, I had to tell them. Although my grandmother was the disciplinarian of the two of them, I also knew that she wore the pants. Grandpa didn't have a say, so I decided to talk to my grandmother alone. When I told her that I was pregnant she told me that it was better to marry than to burn according to the bible and that I needed to prepare to be a wife. She told me that he was a grown man that had created a family and now it was his responsibility to take care of it.

The emancipation began. My mom filed a form with the courts to have me emancipated. This process took months. During the time that we waited for the emancipation, Donnell and I decided to get an apartment and roommate with my older brother's girlfriend who had also just found out that she was pregnant.

Separate from the drama-filled life I was living, there was a special person to whom I always tried to remain close; my father's stepmom. Though I was alone as I passed through many of my struggles, it was here that I often felt the most comfortable. She was no step-grandparent to me. She was the person I felt closest to and knew of my pregnancy. Even though I was 16 and pregnant, we'd still sleep on her small couch together, opposite ends, just like we always had from my infancy whenever I spent the night with her. One morning while I was lounging around the house, I tried calling her. Busy signal. My grandmother felt it was rude to put people on hold, so I thought she must have just been on the other line and I'd catch her a little later.

About an hour later, I received a call from my older brother, DJ. He asked me if I had watched the news. I told him I had not turned the television on. He told me that my grandmother had died. I thought there must have been a mistake. I told him that I had just tried to call her earlier and got a busy signal. He said there had been a fire the night before and that she was found dead inside the house. I was speechless. DJ knew how close we were. She was my best friend. He told me not to go anywhere as he rushed over to get me.

The walls began to close in on me. I felt claustrophobic. She often saved me from having to go to my wicked grandmother's house who had abused me and continued to mistreat me. Her husband had had my father during their marriage, with another woman, and she still accepted me. She spoiled me. I was her baby and now she was gone.

I couldn't stay in the house I needed air, so I went outside to sit on the steps outside my door to wait for my brother. I refused to believe it until I saw the house. As promised, my brother showed up and he drove me past the house so I could see it in person. I thought about the last time I saw her. Donnell had gotten a car and we were driving by her house. She was standing on the porch. She had been asking to meet him, so I asked him to stop. He had refused and kept driving. That was the last time I'd laid my eyes on her living body.

After her funeral, things began to get hard financially. I had been working at McDonald's but one day I felt dizzy and asked to go home. It led to an argument with the manager and that led to me being fired. We couldn't afford to keep up the rent on the apartment and my brother's girlfriend had found out she was pregnant again and was struggling on her end too. So, we decided to let the apartment go. I moved in with Donnell and my mom moved from my grandparent's home back into the house she still owned. Fortunately, my mom only lived a few blocks away from Donnell's mom. Unfortunately, I'd have to walk past the gangs to get from one place to the other.

Donnell lived with his mom, grandfather, his grandfather's 5-year-old daughter, and his sister with her kids. They lived in what I considered the hood, or the ghetto. It was the worst living conditions I had ever been in. They had so many roaches that they kept their toothbrushes in Ziplock bags. I even saw roaches in the refrigerator. I hated living there. Donnell had become more and more distant and never wanted to touch me. He didn't even want to hold my hand in public. I felt rejected. I would beg for intimacy and he would tell me it was a turn-off to be intimate with a pregnant woman. I felt so ugly and unwanted.

Donnell told me that since I was getting married and having a baby, so I had to grow up. He said it was immature of me and unnecessary for me to need to graduate, walk the stage, and go to prom. He said he had experienced it and it was overrated. He suggested that I drop out of high school and just get my GED. Feeling like I had to grow up and be an adult now, I agreed. I never imagined how that decision would affect the rest of my life.

Chapter 9

It's Better to Marry than to Burn

After my grandmother's death, after my class graduated without me, and after missing prom, with Donnell being so distant, I wondered how things could worsen. Of course, I was way ahead of myself. One night, while watching the news, I saw a report of a random shooting in an apartment complex known for its Hispanic gang activity. They reported the incident as a drive-by. This was common, so I didn't think much of it.

About a week and a half later, I found out that the report was about my oldest brother. I went back and forth from Donnell's house to my mom's parent's home. One day, while I was at my grandparent's home, my brother showed up. He was emotional and scared. He wasn't himself. He talked to my uncles and grandfather about his participation in the shooting and they were conflicted about the advice to give him. They couldn't agree on whether or not he should turn himself in. Feeling like he couldn't afford an attorney, he tried to decide the best next step, but time was not on his side. A couple of days later, he was pulled over by the police and arrested.

My grandmother told him she felt like he could plead self-defense considering the details of what happened. She put her house up as collateral to pay for him to obtain a private attorney. To make a long story short, he lost the case, and my only protector was taken away. Because my brother's sentence carried a long term, he wasn't allowed to go to a youth facility, as the judge that sentenced him had suggested. Instead, they sent him to a maximum-security prison, where he was placed on level four, the highest level in the California prison system. Now, I felt completely vulnerable and I was worried about his safety.

During the early part of my pregnancy, I had my first experience of being in danger without my brother. One day, while Donnell and I went shopping downtown, we ran into my brother's girlfriend. She was shopping with her little sister, and she had my nephew with her in the stroller. As we talked in the store, her sister noticed a girl outside. She immediately left the store and my brother's girlfriend followed. We exited the store behind them, not knowing what was going on. Suddenly, her little sister started to fight the girl who was standing there with her friend. My brother's girlfriend left my nephew in the stroller and ran to join her sister in the fight. Donnell grabbed the stroller and I ran to break up the fight as I heard the store owners calling for security.

As I tried pulling my brother's girlfriend off the other girl, she claimed we were jumping her. I tried to explain that I was trying to break up the fight, but she would not hear that. My brother's girlfriend grabbed the stroller, and we all started walking away before security came. The girl that had been fighting my brother's girlfriend kept following Donnell and me as we walked away. She kept trying to fight me. Donnell told me to keep walking. She was getting close and I was afraid that she would attack me from behind. I told Donnell not to let her get to me from behind. He stayed between me and the girl as she continued to follow us. She was on the right side of Donnell and I was on his left. As we continued to try to walk away, she spat past him, right into my face. I blacked out. All I know is I was headed for her! As I ran towards her full speed ahead, suddenly I realized my feet weren't on the ground. As I looked around, I noticed that I was up in the air. Donnell had lifted me above his head. He had picked me up to keep me from reaching the girl and fighting. After spitting in my face, she allowed us to walk away.

I was so pissed off at Donnell. I couldn't believe he allowed that girl to get away with spitting in my face! To make matters worse, he told me that he knew her. He said she was a gangster girl from the hood by his mom's house. From that day on and for the rest of my pregnancy, every time I walked from my mom's house to Donnell's house, I'd have to pass by the home where she and the other gangsters hung out. Donnell was with me most of the time. However, there were times when I'd notice a red beam on my belly. I pointed it out to Donnell, and we knew they were pointing a gun at my belly to intimidate us. Donnell never said a word to the gangsters that bullied me every time I passed them. It was frustrating; I was not only pregnant but I was also getting bullied. I missed my brother. I knew if he were home, this would not be happening.

I was stressed and unhappy. Whenever I tried to initiate intimacy with Donnell, it would result in embarrassing rejection. One night, after we had gone to bed, I tried to get Donnell to show me some affection, but he rejected me again. I got so upset that I told him I was leaving. I got dressed and left his mother's home, headed for my mom's, but halfway there, I saw the gangsters and got scared. I turned around and went back to Donnell's mom's house. As I walked into the room, I found him lying on the bed, watching television without caring. I asked why he didn't come for me when he knew that I would have to walk past the gangsters, and he said, "I knew you'd come back." He had no idea how devastating and belittling that remark made me feel. I felt hopeless. I started to feel like I couldn't live this way for the rest of my life, but I was pregnant, so I stayed, hoping it would get better.

One month after my 17th birthday, exactly one month before my due date, we got a call from the court saying that my emancipation documents had been signed and finalized. I was now considered an adult and free to get married. We had been going to church and were planning to get married as soon as we could. The day we got the call, we went to get the paperwork. We also stopped by the clerk's office to get a marriage certificate. We headed straight to the church where we knew the pastor would be. Donnell had on denim jean shorts and a t-shirt. I had on a cream-colored sweatsuit. My mother and my grandmother went with us to the church. When we arrived, my mom's only brother just so happened to be there and agreed to give me away. We didn't have any money, so we didn't expect a wedding or reception.

After the wedding, we went back to Donnell's mother's house, where they played music, cooked, and everyone danced and celebrated. I didn't have long to go to deliver, so I started spending more time with Donnell at his mom's home. On my due date, I was determined to have the baby. I did not want to be pregnant anymore. I had had preterm labor, and I was happy to make it to my due date, but today was eviction day. I ran up and down the stairs 30 times and did squats. Later that evening, I started feeling contractions. Donnell's car was no longer working, so we had to catch a ride to the hospital. I thought I was ready for delivery.

I arrived at the hospital around 5 p.m. A little while after, the labor pains got stronger. The nurse offered me Demerol for the pain. She explained that it wouldn't take away the pain, but I would be relaxed between contractions. The pain was the worst! I didn't want to go through labor anymore. Maybe it was the medication I'd received, or maybe it was the pain, but for some reason, I thought that if I just left the hospital, my contractions would stop. I told the nurse that I'd changed my mind and decided to stay pregnant. She said "Okay," and left me alone in the room. Donnell had gone to McDonald's to get himself something to eat. I saw this as the perfect time to escape, so I tried getting out of bed with the plan to walk out. As soon as I stood, a contraction hit me, and my knees buckled. I panicked and repeatedly hit the nurse button. The nurse found me crouching on the side of the bed. I was almost on the floor and she panicked. She asked me what I was doing out of bed. I told her I was trying to go to the bathroom. She helped me get back in the bed and told me to call her if I needed to get up again.

My labor lasted for 22 hours. After delivering our son, I was so scared that I didn't have what it took to keep him safe. Taking care of my little brother and sister was different. I would be responsible for this new baby that could easily get hurt and sick. I remember sitting in bed with him on the day we came home from the hospital, thinking that if he could stay alive until he was old enough to get his first round of immunizations, he might have a chance to survive.

It was hard taking care of a baby. My life changed completely. My experience as a young mother felt different from my best friend's, who was able to live her life after having a child at 16 years old. Don't get me wrong, she was still a present and attentive mother, but having older siblings and both parents in the home afforded her more support than I had. For example, her family was in the home when she was released after giving birth and was able to help her with her baby. I went home to Donnell's mom's house, and I had to do everything independently.

Donnell had been attending the local community college. One night when our son was about a week old, I had fallen asleep with the baby before he came to bed. He woke me up and told me that he had seen a mouse run underneath the dresser in our room, the same dresser I got as an infant that my mother had given me for me to use with my baby. I was terrified of mice. He said he just wanted to warn me in case I saw it or heard something while he was at school the next day. I was beside myself in disgust. I had never been in an apartment that had mice. At this point, I was wide awake and afraid. I'd had enough of living with his mom. I stood up from the bed, nothing but a mattress and box spring on the floor, and grabbed my baby. I demanded Donnell take the baby's stroller down the stairs and out to the front porch. I handed him the baby to take downstairs and was mad at him for not carrying me. I ran out of that house and headed for my mom's house. I left the dresser and everything inside of it and never went back.

Our marriage never improved. After our son turned a year old, we decided to rent one of the homes my grandparents owned. It was a four-bedroom home and my mom stayed there with us. The major problem was that all the pimps, gangsters, and drug dealers hung out at the house next door. One day after going grocery shopping, Donnell and I were going back and forth, bringing the bags from the car into the house, when one of the guys from next door walked right up to me in front of Donnell's face and tried to hand me a piece of paper with his name and number on it. I looked down at the paper and walked away. Donnell didn't say a word; he just followed me into the house. I could hear the guys next door laughing as we closed the front door. I was humiliated. I felt like Donnell couldn't protect me. He still never wanted to touch me, and he had not been able to keep a job. I was working and paying all our bills. I didn't want to live like this for the rest of my life. I wanted out! I told Donnell that I wanted a divorce.

My father had left my brother and me a trust fund. It was November, and since I had recently turned 18, I was due to get mine that coming December. I made it up in my mind to leave Donnell and get my place. I used my trust fund money to pay my rent six months in advance to ensure I got approved for the place. I completely furnished the place with all new furniture. Since I was single and didn't like sleeping around with new guys, I thought it would be better to go back to someone I had been with previously. I reconnected with Tyson. I quickly realized that Tyson hadn't changed and was still a cheater. So, I started pulling away. Donnell had moved in with my grandparents after I left him, so he was always around in my business.

When Donnell found out I had seen Tyson again, he got jealous. He began stalking me, saying he wanted to reconcile. I couldn't believe this after all the time I'd begged him for affection and was rejected. That was the last thing on my mind.

One day I got a call from a number I didn't recognize. I answered, and the voice on the other line said, "Hi, baby. I've missed you. I've been looking for you everywhere. I got your number from your sister. How are you?"

It was Dontez. I couldn't believe that he had made so much effort to find me. Being that Tyson had been cheating, I felt single. I agreed to meet up with Dontez. I filled him in on all that had happened since we talked last. He apologized for all the incidents I experienced with other women while talking to him. As we began spending time together, he told me that he was living with his baby's mother but that they were not together. I was not about to fall for that again, so I was very distant and non-committed to Dontez. To entice me to spend time with him, Dontez would do what he did best, spend money on me and shower me with gifts. I continued to spend time with Tyson also.

All was going well. Dontez was giving me a lot of money and I didn't feel like I had to choose one or the other. Plus, I hardly ever saw Dontez. That was until I found out I was pregnant again. I knew it wasn't Dontez's baby, but he was the one giving me money, and I knew he'd be pissed. I was afraid to tell him. When I finally mustered up the courage to tell Dontez, I decided to do it by phone.

All I said was, "I'm pregnant."

He said, "I know it's not mine."

I agreed and he was furious. He told me that he knew the closest person to me in the world was my oldest brother. He said he knew that he was in prison and was connected enough to get him hurt if I didn't get an abortion. I didn't want to get an abortion, but I also believed Dontez had the power to have my brother hurt, and I wouldn't be able to live with myself if he got hurt because of me.

I agreed to do the abortion. Dontez wanted to make sure I went through with it, so he picked me up and took me to my appointment. He said he would be waiting for me to get it done. As I was coming out of anesthesia, I could hear a lady crying very hard. Her cry sounded like mourning. There was a pain heard in the echoes of her moan. I wanted to see who was crying, but I kept dozing back off. As the anesthesia wore off and I became more and more alert, I noticed that the painful dreaded crying I had been hearing was coming from me. I had been crying while unconscious so hard that when I came to myself, I had that heavy breathing cry. The nurse tried to console me, but I just wanted to get out of there.

After I was discharged, the nurses asked me if my ride was waiting for me. I told them that he should be waiting in the waiting room for me. They called repeatedly for my driver, but nobody responded. Dontez had left me there. I called him repeatedly, but he never answered. I had to call my cousin to give me a ride home. I was so embarrassed. After getting home I laid down and just cried. Dontez called me later that night and said something came up and he had to go. I knew I would never talk to him again after threatening my brother's life and making me go through the abortion, then leaving me there. I didn't accept any more calls from Dontez and I told the other guy that I had been seeing that I got rid of the baby and stopped seeing him too. I couldn't believe what I had done. I felt so ashamed and would often have nightmares about the abortion and the baby. I just wanted to forget. I focused on spending time with my son and working.

Chapter 10

From the Pot to the Frying Pan

My older cousin had moved into an apartment with a roommate and started dating a new guy. Her roommate moved out suddenly, and she was looking for a new roommate. I was looking to move as well, so we agreed for me to move in with her, and we'd share the apartment. She told me that her boyfriend had a cousin she wanted to introduce me to. I was skeptical but agreed. We agreed to meet at the apartment. I was ready to escape if I didn't like him.

About 4 p.m., there was a knock on the door. My cousin's boyfriend opened the door, and in walked a very tall, light-skinned, bald guy with freckles and dark circles around his eyes. My cousin's boyfriend Robby introduced me to his cousin.

He said, "Danelle, Edwin. Edwin, Danelle."

I kindly shook his hand and said "Nice to meet you," but in my mind, I was thinking, "He is not my type. What was my cousin thinking?" I was going to be looking for an escape soon. As the night went on, we started playing games and talking and I enjoyed Edwin's sense of humor.

He frequented our apartment, saying he was coming over to visit his cousin, and we began to get closer. A few months later, we were a couple. My cousin and her boyfriend would argue often and things were getting uncomfortable. Edwin had been living with his mother. At the time, I was 19, and he was 22 years old. He said I could move in with him and his mom while we saved money to get our place. I moved in with them, and by March, we'd been together for half a year. Edwin was protective, and even though he didn't have a legal job, he hustled and kept money in his pocket. I found his protectiveness and willingness to hustle attractive after being with Donnell. I didn't recognize his protective nature as controlling in the beginning.

One day after we'd only been together for six months, we went to the music store to get a CD he wanted that had just been released. While in the music store, I recognized one of the employees. He used to date my aunt. He recognized me and we started talking. I called Edwin over and introduced the two. I didn't understand why, but I noticed that Edwin's mood changed. He no longer wanted to look for the CD and he wanted to leave the store immediately. When we arrived back home, he walked into our room first. I followed him and asked him what was wrong, thinking he was upset because he didn't find the CD he wanted. Without a response, he turned to me and backhanded me right across the mouth. I tasted blood immediately. I was shocked! He just slapped me and busted my lip. I started swinging at him, trying to attack him for hitting me.

He grabbed me, and with tears in his eyes, he said he was sorry. He said he didn't know what got into him, that he lost it seeing me talking to another guy in the music store. He said he knew that was my aunt's ex and he had no right to hit me. He apologized over and over and said it would never happen again. That was a lie. That was the beginning of a 7-year abusive cycle. Because time would go by without him hitting me, I always believed him when he said it would never happen again and thought it was the last time.

After being together for a year, we decided to have a baby. We began trying, but month after month, I would get a negative on a pregnancy test. I thought God was punishing me for having the abortion. We moved out of his mom's house and got an apartment. Edwin still didn't work but kept money hustling. I worked and had started going to dental assisting school. Edwin refused to watch my son while I was gone all day, so I had to get up extra early to get him to my grandparent's house before going to school. After dental school in the morning, I'd have to go to the clinic to do my clinical until 4:30 p.m.; then, I had to work from 5 p.m. to 1:30 a.m. I was exhausted. Some mornings I would wake up so tired I'd cry while getting my son dressed to go to my grandparents.

I continued to go to church. One day as I sat there in church hurting from the abuse and exhaustion, I listened to the sermon, and I felt the message was just for me. I found myself at the front of the altar, crying and giving my life to God. I felt so clean and good. I didn't want to do anything to taint that feeling. I told Edwin that I had gotten saved and I was moving out. I happily headed to my grandparent's home, excited about a future with no abuse.

When I got to my grandparent's home, I told my grandmother the decision I had made. I thought she would have been proud of me. Instead, she told me that God didn't work that way. She said that I was going to make Edwin resent God for taking us away and turn him away from God. I felt spiritually obligated not to be why he never turned to God. I hesitantly returned home to Edwin. When I arrived home, he was so happy to see me back. He told me he didn't want to lose me, and that if I were saved and living with him unmarried made me feel like I was betraying God, we'd just get married. I knew I didn't want to marry Edwin, but I felt like it was the right thing to do. I trusted my grandmother and I wanted to please God.

Four weeks later, I sat in the room in the back of the church wearing my all-white wedding dress, trying to get my make-up done, but I couldn't stop crying. I managed to pull myself together and get myself down the aisle. We had moved into a house with a pool in the backyard and we were so low on funds that we decided to have a backyard reception. Before we could take pictures cutting the cake or doing our first dance, Edwin changed into shorts and a t-shirt. I begged him to put his suit back on until the pictures were done, but he refused. In all of our reception photos, I was wearing my wedding dress standing next to Edwin, wearing shorts and a t-shirt.

We continued to try for a baby with no luck. One night I heard that Bishop Noel Jones was visiting a local church. I called Edwin from work and told him that I wanted us to go. To my surprise, when I got home from work, he had his clothes laid out on the bed. At the church service, the bishop talked about our expectations and what we project onto others. He told us that if we have asked

God for something, we had to believe that it would be answered to show faith. He said if we wanted to show faith, we'd tell people that God had already answered the prayer. He then told us to join hands with one person next to us and to pray and ask God for one thing that we were willing to believe him for. Edwin and I joined hands, and coincidentally we both prayed for a baby.

I felt so full after hearing the Word that I just knew I was pregnant that month. I started telling people I was pregnant, and I thought that showed my faith that the prayer was answered. I confidently took a pregnancy test that month and was shocked when I got another negative. I was crushed. I did what the bishop had told me to do. I believed it! What happened? I felt God was punishing me for the abortion and had decided not to bless me with any more children since I took that baby's life. I didn't feel like I deserved a baby after that. I gave up hope.

The next month my cycle was late. My co-worker knew we had been trying and kept encouraging me to test. I told her I refused to test again because it would be negative. She went to the store for her lunch and bought me a pregnancy test. She made me go into the bathroom to take the test. I did it to prove to her that I was right. As I sat on the toilet and peed on the stick, I noticed a second line there that I had not seen before. It came up immediately. I was pregnant! I was so excited that I couldn't finish my shift. My supervisor happily let me go home early. Before going home, I stopped by the drug store to get a card to give to Edwin to let him know.

When I gave him the card, he was so excited! We hugged and danced around the living room. We were so thankful. When I went to my first prenatal appointment, they told me that I was almost two months pregnant. When she told us that, we quickly pulled out a calendar and saw that I had ovulated when we went to the church meeting and got pregnant. It was too early to show on the first test I had taken. I thought this would be the beginning of a better relationship between Edwin and me. I also felt the abuse would stop.

That was wishful thinking.

Edwin continued hitting me throughout my pregnancy. I was so stressed that I went into preterm labor. The doctor put me under strict restrictions and told me to stay on bed rest. He told me he didn't want me to even make a sandwich. I was told only to get up to go from the bed to the couch and to the bathroom. I was told that I could only take a five-minute shower, no longer than ten minutes. Edwin sat right beside me when the doctor explained the danger of losing the baby. The minute we got out of the hospital and into the car, he told me that I knew it was unrealistic to expect to be under the restrictions the doctor just told me I needed to be under.

Edwin expected me to continue to cook dinner, take my son back and forth to school, and keep the house up. His abuse never stopped. One day after he had roughed me around, I started having contractions again. I told Edwin I needed to go to the hospital. He refused to take me and forced me to drive myself the 25 minutes to the hospital, saying he didn't believe I was really in labor. When I arrived at the labor and delivery floor, I was checked immediately. I was, in fact, in labor and was admitted. I was released to return home after a couple of days with strict orders to do the bedrest. I could never do the bedrest as suggested, and I delivered our baby girl four weeks early. Thank God she was healthy.

After the birth of our daughter, the abuse still didn't stop. It only got worse because he expected me to get the baby before she woke him up out of his sleep in the middle of the night, but I had to work the next day, and he didn't. When I'd rebel, I'd get dragged out of bed by my hair and forced to get the baby. Edwin dragged me by my hair so often that there were parts of my hair that stopped growing.

The Christmas after our daughter was born, we attended church together at my grandfather's church. I'd grown up with the members of this church. I had grown up with the assistant pastor's son, and he was there visiting from college. After church, he came up to speak to me and hug me. I introduced him to Edwin, inviting us to hang out with him and his lady friend later. I thought it was a nice offer and looked forward to hanging out together.

As Edwin and I got in the car to leave, I waved goodbye to my family and other church members standing around talking in the parking lot. As we sat at the parking lot's exit waiting for traffic to drive forward, Edwin just lost it.

He said, "How dare you stand right in my face and talk to another man?" He grabbed the brown paper bag that the church had handed out with fruit and candy inside and threw it past my face hitting the window next to me. He then slapped me before I could respond. After slapping me, he attempted to drive out of the parking lot onto the street to leave. My rage hit 10. Even though we were driving, I let out all my rage on Edwin. He started to swerve, and there was a freeway right next to the parking lot we had just pulled out of. Trying to block his head and face from my violent punches, Edwin let go of the steering wheel. We felt the car hit a bump, and Edwin immediately grabbed the wheel and slammed on the breaks.

We were up on the sidewalk about to drive over the freeway overpass onto the freeway when He put the car in reverse while still on the sidewalk and backed into the church's parking lot. My family, uncles, and aunts were all standing in the parking lot watching everything. At the time, our daughter was only about 3-months-old. Edwin grabbed the car seat that she had been strapped in and her diaper bag for protection from my family. He then ran across the street with the baby. I wanted my uncles to kill him and get my baby back. He yelled back at me from across the street that he and the baby would spend the holiday with his ex-girlfriend, and I would get the baby back the next day. That was unacceptable to me. It was my baby's first Christmas. I was breastfeeding, so I panicked.

My aunt grabbed me and said, "Danelle stop crying. You know that man ain't gon' hurt that baby. He's just trying to upset you. He doesn't want that baby, and trust me; he will bring her back."

She had been through a divorce with kids before, so I trusted her. However, I still called his mom and told her what happened, thinking he would go to her house. Sure enough, he had taken my baby to his mom's house. She told him that the baby was breastfeeding and needed to eat and that he better give me my baby back. He listened and brought our daughter home. I hated him. I wouldn't have ever done that to him.

I tried leaving Edwin a few times. I went to my grandparent's house on several occasions, but I felt very uncomfortable there. Grandma's house was everyone's house. I had the kids with me and no privacy. I would only be able to deal with the constant traffic and activity for a short time before going back home to Edwin, and because I was the one paying all the bills; I couldn't save enough to move away from him. Since we thought that getting pregnant with our daughter was a miracle, we were careless with birth control, and I got pregnant when our daughter was about a year old. With another baby on the way, I stayed with Edwin praying things would get better.

My faith and relationship with God grew, and I became spiritually strong. Edwin began to get jealous of the amount of time I was spending at church and reading my bible. He told me that I was not allowed to pay tithes, and I could only go to church two times per week. Our church had taught us that wives are to obey their husbands, so I stopped singing in the choir so that I could go to church on Sunday and bible class on Wednesday nights. The closer I got to God, the more it upset Edwin's demons. He would rarely attend church with us, and one time when he did, we went to night service. In the middle of the service, he decided to leave, but I was not ready to go yet. He told me he was leaving us and we would have to catch a ride home from one of my family members at church. True to his word, he took the car and left us there. I was so embarrassed telling people that my husband left the kids and me with no way to get home or to ask for help.

However, my relationship with God kept getting stronger and stronger. One night Edwin started to pace back and forth, talking mess to me the whole time. I don't even remember what we were arguing about, but I kept quiet. I was cleaning the kitchen before going to bed. I could feel the tension. When you've been in an abusive relationship before, you can spot when it's about to start.

I knew Edwin was trying to aggravate and provoke me to respond with anger so he would have a reason to hit me. But I just ignored what he was saying and started quoting scriptures. I said, "No weapon formed against me shall prosper. Touch not thine anointed and do thy prophets no harm," and I continued.

As I was putting dishes away and quoting scriptures, he got so enraged that he walked right up to me, and as tall as he was, he bent over until he had his forehead touching my forehead, looking me dead in the eyes with his bloodshot eyes. Beads of sweat dripped from his bald head and face, and he gritted his teeth as he spoke. When I looked into Edwin's face, it looked distorted. He didn't look like himself. I saw a wrinkled, disfigured face. I knew it was a demon. I started quoting the scriptures more.

The demon spoke through Edwin and said, "You think because you're quoting scriptures that I won't slap you in your mouth?" I made eye contact with him to let him know that I was not intimidated, and I confidently said, "You can't do anything to me that my God won't allow you to do. And if He allows you to hit me, I'm confident that it will all work for my good. You have no power over me."

I thought for sure he'd slap me then. I braced myself. But God held his hand. He just walked away, and it ended for the night. For the first time, when he was this upset, he didn't hit me! God had given me a loving gift that showed me He was there and would never leave me.

Chapter 11

I've Healed Too Much to Let You Keep Beating Me

When you are in an abusive relationship where the abuser is physically taking out their frustrations of inferiority on you, it can be quite hard to find your way out. You want to believe that they are really sorry this time and that the last time they hit you is the last, but that is hardly ever the case. I went through a 7-year relationship where I was physically abused. He had me thinking that all the women wanted him and that if I lost him, I could be replaced in a second with someone better that he wouldn't have to beat. Coupled with my previous abuse, the abuse that I endured at his hands had me believing that if I gave up on him, I would miss out on him being a better man and all that he had to offer. I didn't want to believe that I would go through all of that for nothing, only for him to have learned his lesson and give everything I wanted to someone else.

When our daughter was about two years old, and before our son turned one, they both fell ill. They had an extreme case of diarrhea. My personal experience, almost dying from dehydration from diarrhea as a baby, meant that I knew the severity of the situation. We rushed them to the ER, and they placed us in a small room with both babies. They told us not to give them a bottle because every time they drank, it caused them to pass fluids again.

It was difficult to get them settled down. Edwin had our daughter in the bed, and I sat in the chair holding our infant son. We finally got them to sleep when Edwin told me that I needed to get up to change our daughter's diaper because she had pooped. I told him that our son was sleeping on my chest, and if I moved, he would wake up, and it would be hard to get him back to sleep. He snapped at me, "I don't give a fuck!" he said, Get up and change her now!" I obeyed and gave our son to him and changed our daughter.

Unsurprisingly, our son woke up and, once again, got fussy. Edwin didn't have the patience to handle him, and I knew it wouldn't be long before I would have to get him. I had to lay there ignoring my son as he cried and struggled because I was exhausted, and I wanted to get a little bit of sleep. Just as I began to doze off, I heard Edwin yelling at me to get up and get the baby because he couldn't get him to settle down. Frustrated, I told Edwin that I had warned him that this would happen and that he was going to have to get him to settle down.

He said, "Bitch, if you don't get up and get this baby, I will leave you all here!"

I knew he'd leave us, and then I'd have to handle them both alone. Of course, I conceded and got up to get the baby. I sat in that chair and struggled to get our son back to sleep while I watched Edwin climb in bed with our daughter and fall right to sleep.

After a couple of hours, the kids were released from the hospital. We got home late, and I tried to get some sleep before work the next day. Edwin would drive me to work, even though he didn't have a job, because we only had one car, and he didn't want to be without transportation all day. The next day while he was driving me to work, I felt like I was in a daze. I was so tired and emotionally exhausted. I had been up with the babies all night by myself. I don't even remember the argument, but Edwin was going off about something, and before I knew it, he had backhanded me in the mouth again and busted my lip. I was so tired that I didn't even flinch or respond. I just sat there and swallowed the blood.

As I entered the office and walked to my desk, I felt like a zombie. I had lost my smile. I was still praying for deliverance, but I had lost myself. There was a Hispanic lady that sat across from my cubicle that was just a little older than I was. She looked me dead in my face and made eye contact with me as I sat down. She saw the busted lip and the blood. As we locked eyes, the tears began to roll down my face. She got up and came over to my desk, and put her arms around me. She handed me a tissue and sat in front of me to block the view of others around. She didn't have to ask what happened. We both understood that she knew.

She told me that she was living in an apartment complex in a good neighborhood and that the unit next door to her had just become available. She said that she had a good relationship with the manager, and she believed that if she referred me, I'd be approved. I doubted it would work out, but I asked her how I could apply. She called the manager, and the manager agreed to accept my application via fax. The manager faxed the application to our office. I filled it out and faxed it right back. I got a call back before the end of the day at work and was told that I was approved. I was so excited. This opened my eyes to the possibility of a way out.

But how could I do it?

I had no money saved. I was also afraid Edwin would be able to convince me not to go. Also, the apartment wouldn't be ready for a couple of weeks. So, I kept it to myself.

One day while at home, Edwin was having a bad day. He began pumping himself up again to start a fight with me. As usual, I saw it coming. I began to think about how I dreamed of being married one day and what my family would look like. After all that dreaming about what my life would look like when I grew up and found someone to love me, I was left with nothing that made me feel secure or safe at all. I felt like Sofia in The Color Purple when she spoke the famous quote, "All my life I had to fight. I had to fight my daddy. I had to fight my uncles. I had to fight my brothers. A girl child isn't safe in a family of men, but I ain't never thought I'd have to fight in my own house! I love Harpo, and God knows I do. But I'll kill him dead before I let him beat me."

Everyone has a limit and can only take so much.

I was standing at the sink washing dishes. I let the water run so it could get as hot as it could. After it got scalding hot, I put a pot under the water and let it begin to fill as he continued to walk back and forth, talking mess. As expected, he came up to me and grabbed me by my throat. He choked me for a few seconds and then let me go. As he proceeded to walk away, I grabbed the pot of scalding water out of the sink and threw it on him. He had a bald head and was wearing a wife-beater. He turned around, and all I saw was a fire in his eyes. He approached me and immediately grabbed me by my neck. He choked me again for a few seconds and let me go. As he proceeded to walk away this time, I grabbed the mop. I held the mop by the end and swung the stick so hard I heard it cut through the wind! It hit him directly on the right side of his bald head! Bingo! But he was still conscious. He grabbed me, and we tussled around the kitchen. He had me by my throat, this time with both his hands, and I really couldn't breathe. He had me bent over the kitchen slab where our house phone was usually placed. I had a quick flash and thought that this man didn't realize how hard he was choking me. I thought to myself, "He is going to kill me!" Then the thought came that if he killed me, he would panic and probably kill the kids and himself too.

The thought of that made me blackout. All I remember after that was grabbing the phone to call 9-1-1, but when I grabbed it, he let go of my neck with one hand to grab the phone from me. I saw the arm stretched across my face, and I bit it! I bit it until I tasted his blood in my mouth! The next thing I remember is coming to myself and seeing my children standing in the hallway, watching me. He was on the floor in the living room with his hands covering his face, with one leg stretched out, screaming my name while I was beating him with the lamp from our living room. I knew then that if I didn't leave, I would either kill him and end up in prison, then my kids would not have any parents, or he would kill me.

That was it! I made up my mind to leave. I told him that I was leaving in one week. He didn't believe me at first. After the incident, everything began to feel perfect, but I didn't fall for it. I finally evaluated the reason that I had always come back to him after being beaten. The reason that I'd always go back was that, when leaving him, I'd go to my grandparent's house, which was home to EVERYONE! It was uncomfortable for me and my children, so we would only stay long enough for me to get back on my feet. The fact of the matter was, I'd rather deal with being in my own home where my children had their own rooms than subject them to having to live with my grandparents.

I realized the reason I went to my Grandparent's place as my temporary escape was because I was the one paying all the bills. So, I decided to stop paying the bills for a month and put it towards finding a place for us to move to. I moved in without any furniture. I was so happy to finally be able to sleep without the worry of being dragged out of bed by my hair. My co-worker helped me a lot. Her family donated furniture to me, and I could care less if it matched. I was tasting life without abuse again.

The apartment was a three-bedroom, two-bathroom, single-level, one-story apartment with a nicely-sized patio. My kids loved it there. Edwin would come around to visit the kids, but we were not a couple. He had moved in with one of his friends so he could pay the bills I'd left him with. I was happy.

Our daughter fell sick right before Christmas that year. She had just turned three years old. She had a cold, and I'd taken her to her doctor and was told it would pass. She kept complaining about her tummy hurting. She also had asthma, so when she had breathing problems, I gave her a breathing treatment. I thought the tummy pain was just gas, so I treated it with gas drops. But her abdominal pain got worse. It got so bad that she would wake up out of her sleep and start screaming in pain shouting, "Mommy! Mommy! My tummy!"

Finally, it got so bad that nothing would help relieve her. Since she had been sick, Edwin decided to stay over with us that night. We rushed her to the ER. When we arrived, we were sat in the waiting room and told to wait. She was taking short, shallow breaths, and she was coughing up white foam. We sat there so long that the sun had risen, and we realized her doctor's office was open. We decided to leave the ER and take her to see her doctor.

When we arrived at her doctor's office, he examined her immediately. I knew something was wrong when he rushed out of the room and started calling for the nurse. I could hear him through the door demanding that the nurse get the ER on the line stat. Once the doctor was on the line with the ER's charge nurse, I heard him tell her, "My patient was just there in the ER and had been waiting all night to be seen. This child is only three years old, and her right lung has collapsed, and her left lung is only operating at about 50%. I am sending them back to the ER, and I expect that they will be seen immediately!"

We were terrified. I felt like I should have known. How could I have been treating her with gas drops and breathing treatments? Our baby had pneumonia! After being examined by the hospital doctor, we were told that pneumonia had eaten little holes in her right lung. She was placed in ICU, and we really were not given any guarantees that she would improve.

One night while I lay with her in ICU, holding her as she cried from the pain, she asked me to have my grandfather come to pray for her. She had built a close bond with my grandfather. I called my grandparents, thinking he would just pray for her over the phone, which he did. As we were dozing off to sleep, the nurse rang our room. She said we had visitors. I looked at the clock, and it was 1 'o'clock in the morning. I thought, who in the world could it be? The nurse said it was my grandparents. I was shocked and told her to let them in. I'll never forget the power I saw as my grandfather and grandmother entered the room. My grandfather was using his cane with one hand and holding my grandmother's hand with his other hand. On the other hand, she held a bottle of blessed oil. I said, "You guys didn't have to come all the way down here." My grandfather responded with, "My baby called and asked me to pray for her. I told your grandma to get up, get dressed, and take me down to that hospital."

He felt the need to lay hands on her. After we prayed for her, he kissed her and left. Edwin was a mess while she was in the hospital. He told me that he went to church and told God that he wanted his family back. He said he was baptized and promised God that if He spared our daughter's life, he would do right by us going forward. I didn't believe Edwin, and I certainly didn't want to go back to him. I had stayed faithful in the church. Edwin went to my pastor and told him about his request to God and about my hesitation. He asked the pastor to speak with me.

When the pastor spoke with me about Edwin's request, I told him flat out that he beats me. My pastor told me that he believed Edwin was sincere and told me he felt like the enemy was trying to trick me into being single so he could devour me. He said that he would mentor him to help keep him on track but suggested that I reconcile. I was still not confident enough in myself to trust my own decisions. I felt it was not proper to disobey the pastor's advice. Our daughter improved and was released from the hospital right before Christmas.

I took my pastor's advice and reconciled with Edwin. We moved out of my apartment and into a house. I doctored up his resume and got him a management job at a group home. The house was beautiful in a neighborhood that we had once dreamed of living in. It was a new home with vaulted ceilings. There was a grassy area across the street where the kids would be able to ride their bikes. We would even take family walks through the neighborhood, and things seemed to be good for a short while. Although Edwin and I argued, he didn't hit me again after the day I beat him. He carried our daughter to bed every night, and she loved having him back in the house.

One night while we were all sleeping, I woke up for no apparent reason. I rolled over and looked beside me and noticed that Edwin was not in bed. Then I heard banging on the door. It was about 2 a.m., and whoever it was, they were demanding that we open the door. I knew Edwin kept a gun in the house and assumed shortly I would hear him answer the door. After no answer, they banged again. I was annoyed, afraid they would wake up the kids, and I wondered where Edwin was. I jumped out of bed and grabbed my robe. I headed down the hall to the door as I threw my robe on, trying to tie it quickly. Edwin saw the bedroom light come on and came running down the hall to meet me. I thought something was wrong, but he told me to go back to bed. I asked him who was at the door, and he said he didn't know who it was. He said that by the time he got to the door, they were gone.

I did not believe this story because he was already out of bed when I woke up, and they were still banging on the door. Knowing his character, I felt that if he didn't know who was at the door, he would've answered it with his gun. He did not allow unexpected visits from anyone to our home. I assumed in my mind that it must have been a woman. I resolved that he must have been outside with her, or she knew where he lived and came to our home. Maybe they were arguing, and he was trying to get her to leave before I found out she was there. I had no proof of this, and he denied it, so I had to let it go. But I put a pin in it. That was my way of not addressing it right away, but not forgetting it either.

After working at my job for four years, I was let go. For the first time, I was dependent on Edwin. And to make matters worse, I had gotten pregnant immediately after we reconciled. One night, my best friend and I had plans to hang out. Edwin said that he would be hanging out with his friends so we left the kids at my mother's. My best friend had broken her toe, so instead of going somewhere that required her to walk around, we decided to just cruise around for a relaxing drive and see the city life.

While we were driving around and listening to music, she got a call from her boyfriend. I could tell from her responses that he was accusing her of lying to him about being out with me. He told her that he had just seen me in the club with my husband. I took the phone from her and asked him if he was sure he had seen my husband. Once he noticed that she was not lying to him and that I was, in fact, with her, he wanted to back out of what he had said he saw. I pressured him into telling me what he had seen, what he saw my husband wearing, and where he saw him.

After he told me what I wanted to know, my best friend and I headed to the club where my husband was seen with another woman. My best friend could not walk, so she dropped me off on the corner by the club and told me to call her if I needed a ride home. It was almost 2 a.m., so I knew the club was about to close. I waited for everyone to start exiting. There he was, exiting the club with some black girl with a huge booty, hanging on his arm. They were smiling at each other as they began walking to the corner across from me.

Edwin didn't notice me crossing the light to meet him at the corner as he approached it with his date. By the time he noticed me, I was right up on them. His date was still hanging onto his arm. I walked up to them and held my hand out for her to shake it.

I introduced myself and said, "Hi, I'm his wife, and you are?"

She looked at me and smiled as if she was not surprised. Edwin just stood there staring at me. I noticed him trying to discreetly push her arm off of him.

Edwin responded to me by telling me that she was his friend. The crossing light turned green, and it was time for us to cross. When my best friend and I had pulled up to the club, I'd noticed his car there. I also saw his friends driving away in a different truck, so I knew he wasn't riding with them. I asked him if they were leaving together. The girl responded first. She said, "No, I'm going my own way."

Edwin looked at me and said, "I need to take her home." My shocked expression said it all.

I said, "In our car?" This conversation was going on as we all walked in the direction of his car. By the time I asked him if he planned on putting that girl in our car to take her home, we had almost reached the front of his car.

Parked right beside Edwin's car were my best friend's cousin and her friends. She saw me and noticed what was going on. She jumped out of the car to my defense. The girls immediately started pressuring Edwin's date. He wanted to get her out of there ASAP. He blocked her from the attack and put her in his car and drove off, and left me, his newly pregnant wife, standing there in the middle of the street.

My best friend's cousin gave me a ride home. I immediately jumped in my car, trying to find him. The first place I thought to look for him was his mother's house. While I drove there, I blew his phone up. He answered, but I could tell he was just trying to bide time. He knew I was on my way. I arrived at his mother's house, ran to the door, and surprisingly, she was awake. She told me that I had just missed Edwin. That he rushed off. I told her how I had just caught him with a girl at the club.

She allowed me to go check his room. Upon entering his room, I saw an empty condom wrapper on the floor. I took it to show to his mother. She said he must have taken the girl out of the back door before he left out the front door because he knew she wouldn't have allowed him to bring another girl to her home. I had no idea where he could have gone. I went home and began calling every hotel in town, asking for a guest by his name. I did not locate him. When I ran out of numbers to call, I sat there in the dark, alone, and cried from a place that was deeper than I had ever felt.

I don't know when I fell asleep, but when I woke up, I felt wet. I looked down, and I was covered in blood. I drove myself to the hospital and soon, I was laying in the ER bed alone in the dark. The doctor came in and informed me that the baby had no heartbeat. They directed me to follow up with my prenatal doctor and discharged me to go home. I still hadn't heard from Edwin. I went home like Angela Bassett in Waiting to Exhale! I took all his clothes and belongings and threw them outside onto the front lawn. I took a big 8 by 10 picture of him that had been hanging on the wall down and nailed it to the tree outside, and put up a sign that read, "Caught-Husband Cheating Sale. Everything is free!" I took his suede dress shoes and put them underneath the dripping faucet by the front porch. I went back inside and waited to hear from him.

When Edwin came home to find his things outside, he was pissed. I expected him to be remorseful and beg for forgiveness. I told him about losing the baby, and he told me that he needed two weeks to decide which one of us he wanted. He said in the meantime to expect him to go back and forth. Sometimes he'd stay the night at home and sometimes he may not come home. I thought he had lost the little bit of mind that God gave him.

His phone started ringing. He answered it. It was her. She wanted to know how long he would be before returning to her. He told her he was grabbing a change of clothes and he would be back shortly. I was in shock.

About a day or so later, the kids and I arrived home after running errands. When I pulled into the driveway, I noticed his car was there. As the children and I entered the house, he walked out of the back bedroom with the girl I'd seen him with at the club.

My kids and I just stood there. I wanted to grab her and act a fool, but I didn't want my kids to go through witnessing that. He told us that they were just there grabbing a few of his things, and they would be leaving soon. After they left, I convinced the phone company that his phone had been stolen and I needed to update his access password. After getting access to change his password, I had the ability to control his phone remotely. I updated his outgoing messages to a personal message from me where I informed all of his callers that I had caught him with another woman and that I had taken over his phone. I advised them to leave a message, and if I felt it was important enough to relay to him, I would.

He was humiliated. Turning his phone off didn't help. All it did was redirect all of his callers to a voicemail where they'd find my lovely outgoing message. Besides, I had already set all of his calls to go to voicemail automatically anyway. I was enjoying his humiliation. People kept calling his phone just to hear the message and laugh. How did I know? Because they'd listen to it all the way through until the voicemail would pick up, and before they hung up, you'd hear them laughing and making comments.

When I refused to give Edwin access to his phone back, his girl called me. She told me she went by the name of Barbie. I asked her if she had known about me and she said yes. She told me that before I lost my job, she'd be at my house having sex with Edwin in our bed after I had gone to work. She sarcastically told me that she told Edwin to change the sheets, but he refused, saying I would notice. In an attempt to prove that he cared for her more, she went on to tell me how she loved the Gucci boots that were in my closet. She said that Edwin had told her she could have them, but they weren't her size.

I asked her if she knew that I was pregnant. She said yes, she found out, and that is why they were arguing the night she was banging on the door. So, I was right! I asked her, sister to sister, black woman to black woman, how she could do this knowing he was married, had children with me, and had a baby on the way. She quickly interrupted me and told me that Edwin had already told her that our baby had died. She told me that they had been trying to get pregnant, and she thought they might have actually been successful. She said she also loved my home and was planning to move in when I moved out.

I was appalled. Since I had lost my job and Edwin's job didn't offer benefits, I was still carrying our deceased baby a week after finding out it was dead. I was miserable. I couldn't afford to pay for the procedure to get the baby out, and because all of the agencies looked at how much money I made prior to the current month, I was denied assistance. I had a follow-up appointment with my OB/GYN a week after the baby died. When he found out that I was still carrying the baby, he said he would do a D&C free of charge that day.

Although Edwin accompanied me to the appointment and the hospital for the outpatient procedure, Barbie was blowing his phone up the entire time, and he kept stepping out to take her call. Before being wheeled back into the surgery room, I asked Edwin to please be close by, and there for me when the surgery was over. All I could think about was how I was left after the abortion by Dontez. I asked him to please spend the time that I was in surgery praying for me to come through safely and to deal with Barbie after I was discharged. He agreed.

After the procedure was completed, I was taken to the recovery room. The nurses began calling for Edwin to join me there, but he was nowhere to be found. The nurses actually walked the halls looking for him, and finally, one nurse found him tucked away from the visiting room on the phone with Barbie. He dropped me off at home and left to go spend the night with Barbie.

I vented to an old friend about what I was going through and how I had no job. I was told that I could be referred for an opening at the office where they worked. I went in and was hired on the spot. I started a day after I had the procedure. I went in on my first day without an ounce of sleep. I had spent the night taking the painkillers in hopes that they would make me drowsy, but all I did was lay in bed crying.

One night, Edwin decided to stay the night at home. He said Barbie lived with her family, and it was not peaceful or comfortable, and he needed a good night's rest. As he lay there sleeping peacefully, I stayed beside him, watching him and thinking about how much I hated him. I was disgusted at how peacefully he slept after all he had done to me. I felt like he had the nerve to think he was safe.

Edwin must have felt me staring at him because he woke up and was shocked to see me looking him right in his face.

He said, "What's going on?"

I calmly responded by saying, "Nothing. I'm just sitting here thinking about how you think it's cool to sleep next to me after all you've done. I was thinking about how I want to kill you, bury your body in the backyard, and call the police to tell them I did it while having a cigarette over your dead body. And the only thing that I'm second-guessing is having a cigarette because I don't smoke. I would plead temporary insanity, and I think I would have a good case considering all that I have dealt with."

Edwin slowly began to climb out of bed. He grabbed his clothes, never taking his eyes off of me. I didn't budge or say a word. I just stared right back into his eyes.

Edwin left that day and never spent another night in our home. He moved back in with his mother. He also stopped helping me financially. Since I had just gone back to work and hadn't gotten paid yet, I was broke. The water had been cut off and we needed to move. Edwin refused to help at all. Where would I go with my children? I cried and couldn't believe that I listened to the pastor, and this is where I ended up. Where was he and all his mentoring for Edwin that he promised? Come to think of it, he had only gone to breakfast with Edwin once! How could a man of God have been so wrong? I wished I had never listened to him and reconciled with Edwin.

One night as I lay in the house with no running water, I cried out to God. I asked him why he allowed me to go through so much. I asked him why he let things get so bad. I felt the presence of God enter the room. I felt led to grab my bible. I didn't search for a scripture; I just opened the book. It opened to a story found in Acts 27. I began reading about a storm that a ship had gone through. The part that stood out to me began at verse 39.

Acts 27:39

When daylight came, they did not recognize the land, but they saw a bay with a sandy beach, where they decided to run the ship aground if they could. Cutting loose the anchors, they left them in the sea and at the same time untied the ropes that held the rudders. Then they hoisted the foresail to the wind and made for the beach. But the ship struck a sandbar and ran aground. The bow stuck fast and would not move, and the stern was broken to pieces by the pounding of the surf.

I felt a gentle spirit speaking to me, saying, "Daughter, you asked me to deliver you from this abusive relationship, but you kept finding a reason to go back. Just like the ship in the story, I had to tear the past up so much that you could not get back on that boat for any reason. Me allowing it to get this bad was to ensure you would never look back."

That night as I slept, I had a very vivid dream that, to this day, I have never forgotten. As I fell into a deep sleep for the first time in days, I woke up in an old house. Edwin was there, and he was standing over me as I lay on the floor against an old bed with an old quilt on it. The house was dark. Sheets were hanging in the bedroom doorway for privacy, taking the place of where a door should have been. I was bleeding from my mouth, and my clothes had been torn. It was obvious that I looked the way I did because of a beating that I had just gotten from Edwin. Edwin started heading out of the room towards the front door, and on his way out, he demanded that I not leave the house.

I watched out of the window as Edwin drove away. I saw the back of his car turn the corner, and I ran out the doorway looking for help. The street was bare and dark and the sky was a gloomy gray. Nobody was outside, but the neighborhood looked very familiar. That's it. I was back on the street where my paternal grandmother was. By now, in real life, my grandmother had died, and I hadn't been back to that neighborhood in years.

I began to walk down the street to see if I could find anyone. I came across an old house. It looked like a slave house in movies, made from wood, with a long porch that wrapped around the house. There was a tall tree in the front yard. I saw an old lady sitting in a rocking chair on the porch, wearing an old long dress that looked like she had made it herself. Her hair was all wrapped up in a scarf. She held a baby in her arms that was completely wrapped in a blanket.

I approached her yard. I told her how I'd just been beaten by my husband, and I needed help. She just kept rocking in her chair as she listened. After I had poured out my heart, she stood up and told me to follow her into the house. She sat in another rocking chair in the middle of her modest living room. She continued to rock this baby that she held in her arms, and in my spirit, I felt like that was the baby I had aborted.

I told the old lady how I had grown up without my father, how my brother had been taken to prison, and I felt alone and unprotected. She began talking and telling me how many had passed onto the next life, and people in this life would judge how they lived and conclude that they went to Hell. She started telling me stories of people I knew that had died and I'd assumed were going to hell. As she told their stories, they appeared on the couch next to me.

When she finished, I was confused. I thought all of that was good, but I didn't feel like I had what I needed, a protector.

I kindly told her, "I appreciate you telling me these things and seeing all of you, but I really want to see my dad."

The old lady looked at me and said, "There he is."

As she turned her head to look towards the opposite end of the couch from me, I followed her eyes over all the people sitting next to me, and sure enough, at the end of them all, there was my father. We both stood up, and I ran into his embrace. It felt so real. He was wearing an all-white suit with an all-white tie that was so clean and appeared like he was glowing. His hair was in a perfectly picked-out afro. My father had a very fair complexion and high cheekbones. He wasn't very tall. I'd say only about 5'11, give or take an inch. Although he had died from being burned all over his body, he didn't have a mark on him. He was just like I had pictured him. He looked just like my older brother!

Everyone that had been sitting on the couch got up and went out to the front yard. I cried on my father's chest and began to tell him how much I had missed him and how sorry I was for praying that he would go away. He put his arm around my shoulder, and we began to walk towards the front door to join the others outside. As we walked, he told me that he loved me, my brother, and our mother. He said it was not his will for our lives to turn out the way they did. He told me not to worry about my brother in prison and told me that he was there with him. He told me that he wanted better for me and that I had it in me to do better for myself. He told me not to give up.

As we stepped out on the porch, I saw rays of light shining down from the Heavens. Everyone was standing in the front yard singing and dancing under the big tree. I told my father that I wanted to stay with him. It felt so good to be with him, and everything was so peaceful. My father looked me in the eyes and told me that I had to go back home but to know that he would be with me. He kissed my forehead, jumped off the porch, and joined the others dancing and singing. As I began to walk away, back towards the house, my father called my name. I looked back, he had the biggest smile on his face. The sky beamed with the most beautiful sunrise I had ever seen in my life, and my father said, "This is how we worship in Heaven."

I smiled and turned to walk away.

When I arrived back at the house where Edwin had left me, I saw police cars and lights. As I entered the house, there was a big, tall, dark man wearing a trench coat questioning Edwin and telling him that he knew he had been abusing me. I was taken aside as the man handcuffed Edwin and began escorting him out of the house and placing him under arrest. As the man passed by me, he made eye contact with me, smiled, and winked. At that moment, I knew it was my dad in another body. That made me feel comfortable knowing that my dad was always around watching over us, even when I couldn't see him.

The next morning, when I awoke from my dream, I knew my life had changed, and it no longer included Edwin. I decided to tell Edwin to forget about the two weeks he had requested to decide if he wanted Barbie or me and make it a lifetime with her because he was no longer welcome back in my life. I prayed and decided to go back to the apartment complex that I had moved out of when I reconciled with Edwin to see if they would help me. I spoke with the same manager that I had always dealt with. I explained what had happened and how I had no money and no place to go. God gave me favor with that woman and she gave me the keys to the only apartment they had available immediately. I had no money to give her but she said it was ok. She told me that I had never been late before, and she would work with me to catch up. It was a two-bedroom apartment, and all my kids would have to share a room, but we wouldn't be homeless.

I refused to go to the pastor of the church I'd been attending who gave me such horrible advice, so I asked some of the brothers from my grandfather's church if they would help me move. Due to the water being turned off, I couldn't clean the house before moving out. We had dirty dishes in the sink, and the ants had started to gather. Ashamed to let the brothers inside and see how dirty the house was, I was determined to have all the furniture and things we planned to take moved to the front yard before they arrived. My oldest son was nine years old at the time. He and I moved everything out of the house. When the brothers arrived, they were shocked that we had done all that work by ourselves. They moved everything into our new apartment, and my life was finally starting over.

Chapter 12

LIVING LIFE AFTER ABUSE

Of the people who go through abusive relationships, some turn bitter and cold, some shut down and lose all sexual desire, while others become insatiable and promiscuous; the latter is often just a cry to be truly loved. They feel that since their body is all anyone has ever valued, that means it is all they have to offer. As I stated earlier, only hurt people hurt other people, and this vicious cycle continues in our present communities and the generations to come. But not all hurt people hurt people. I wanted to be one that learned from my experiences.

The word *forgiveness* is now being thrown around like the latest cliché. Many don't really experience the peace of real forgiveness. Many don't know what real forgiveness looks or feels like. Forgiveness can be tested by how a person feels when the person that offended them comes around or is mentioned. It is not always seen in how they outwardly respond but in how they feel inside. You must be willing and mature enough to be honest with yourself, to experience true forgiveness.

When someone is unable to forgive, they are bound by the memories of the offense. Whenever the memory is triggered, they have an internal reaction. Anything that can alter how you are feeling has control over you. If you are not in control of yourself, how can you boast about how great you are, and how would you feel capable of controlling others? The first step in mastering anything is mastering self.

It's not always easy to forgive. Especially if the offender has not expressed any remorse or if you know they will repeat the offense. After all Edwin had done, I found it very difficult to forgive him. But forgiveness doesn't mean you have to leave yourself vulnerable to being betrayed, abused, or taken advantage of. Our Savior is not weak. He has a merciful side and a side of judgment. When His word tells us to forgive, He is referring to the act of not holding any grudges, not being bound by the offense, nor being so focused on the offense that your flow of love is blocked, and the offense becomes your why.

How many times have you asked someone why they did something and they said because someone else did something first? I was told as a child that two wrongs don't make a right. When my cousins and I would fight, my grandmother would say that she didn't care who got the first lick. She would get the last and get everyone that got a lick in the fight. You cannot control the actions of others. You also cannot let the actions of others control you. Being your best requires not reducing yourself to a lower vibration based on the circumstances you've been dealt with.

We are not justified to do wrong because wrong was done to us. That is why the bible tells us to treat others the way we would want to be treated, not the way we are treated. God does not teach us to value the eye-for-an-eye way of living. There is a reason that you went through what you went through. The only way to stop the lesson from repeating itself is to learn what you need to learn from the experience, so you won't have to go through it again. God does not allow us to go through things because He enjoys watching us struggle. He knows the right amount of disappointment, success, rejection, loss, illness, isolation, and joy that you need to produce what e created for you to produce. That is why we can rest in peace that surpasses all understanding. That is why we don't have to get even when we are wronged.

All things work for the good of those who love God and are called according to His purpose. When you can accept this, you will stop thinking that everything that happened to you was from the devil, and he must be stopped. He can do nothing that God doesn't allow, and if God loves you and allows it, can you trust Him through it? You will be amazed at how much you grow in your darkest hour. When you see the lesson in the experience, you are able to be grateful to have gone through it instead of being bound by shame, guilt, and depression. You will also be able to forgive the offender because it's no longer about them.

With true forgiveness, letting go, and moving on, the possibility that the pain you are experiencing now will not last is born. It births the possibility that your future was designed to look better than your past or what you're currently still trying to hold on to. God wants us to learn how to trust Him enough to let go and know that when we must let something go, it's because something greater is in store.

I heard a story once, and I may not tell it accurately, but I want to give you the message.

There was a little girl whose father would tuck her in every night. One day, as she and her father passed by a store, the little girl saw a string of fake pearls on display. She was drawn to the necklace and asked her father if she could have it. He told her that she'd have to earn it, which she did. Once she earned enough to buy the pearls, her father took her to the store to buy them. She loved those pearls and swore to never take them off. One night while her father was tucking her into bed, he kissed her head and asked her, "Do you love Daddy?" The little girl replied, "Of course, Daddy, I love you!" The father said, "Give Daddy your pearls." Surprised at the request, the little girl clutched her pearls and said, "Oh, Daddy… not my pearls. I will give you my favorite stuffed animal. You know I've had this since I was born." The father just smiled at her and said, "No baby, you keep your stuffed animal. Daddy loves you. Goodnight." He kissed her and left the room. The next night the same thing happened. This time the little girl offered him all of the money out of her piggy bank instead of giving him her pearls. The father just smiled at her and said, "No baby, you keep your money. Daddy loves you. Goodnight." He kissed her and left the room. On the third night, while the father was tucking her in, she said, "Daddy, I've been thinking. I love you more than my pearls. So, if you want them, you can have them, Daddy." The father smiled at her and told her that he loved her and asked her to close her eyes and hand him the pearls. As she did, he placed a real pearl necklace in her hand. Sometimes we are holding on to imitations of things we say we want out of the fear that we might not get the real things we seek. Really, we don't trust God's plan to give us better results than we are able to achieve doing it our way. We settle, thinking that doing things our way will secure us our best results. This shows that we have not submitted to God's power and will for our lives. In this mindset, we are doubting God and trying to treat God as our personal genie.

If God said something is for you, then you don't have to hold on as if you will lose it. If God is telling you to release something, it's because there is something else better. If God closes a door, you don't have to despair as if you lost the best thing you could have ever gotten. God's plan for you is always the best possible outcome. Not trusting in Him and His plan is where you fall short and feel incomplete inside. The more you trust God, the more He will prove to you that there is no one above Him and nobody could love you better or offer you more.

When you experience Godly forgiveness, you break chains that the enemy thought would keep you bound. Only in true forgiveness are you able to love your enemies. You are spiritually led on what boundaries to set that are not vindictive, malicious, or selfishly motivated. You experience true happiness that can't be taken away by those who seek to destroy you. In learning to forgive my ex, I learned to forgive myself. I began to see that I could enjoy life again, and this time it would not be founded on the love I get from a man. With this forgiveness, I wouldn't be bound by bitterness, and I would be able to love again if I ever decided to.

When you're motivated by love and live in your purpose and transparency, you live in true freedom. Be the real un-watered-down, God-designed you. Becoming the best version of yourself is becoming what you were designed to be. Anything being used outside of the manufacturer's original purpose is an abuse of the product. If you do not know your purpose, I will bet my last dollar that you are abusing yourself. Operating outside of the original design is a malfunction.

On my journey to being the best me, I started out being motivated by wanting my ex to see and love me. I came to realize that one cannot truly become their best through holding onto shame and changing what things look like to others on the outside. I became that person that I could really love, and it transformed my desires. Once my desires had changed, I had no choice but to change my boundaries, which only left room for what I wanted and needed.

The lowest day of my life became the greatest day I can remember. When you tell your story to impact others, they won't be concerned with your success, they will want to know about your valley and how you made it out. They want to know if it is something they can mimic. That's why transparency is one of the greatest tools when the mission is to inspire, impact, and change the lives of others.

I was bound by shame. I knew I'd have to face the gossip about me being under 25, twice divorced, with three kids by two different men. I was embarrassed and wanted to isolate myself, but I decided to press forward. When you are not confident, and shame is affecting your decisions, you usually avoid others and isolate yourself so you won't have to feel the shame. There is no growth in this type of isolation. This shame is rooted in comparing ourselves to others that we think are better than us. If we knew what those that we put on a pedestal did in private, we would not feel so ashamed about our own flaws and shortcomings. Even your pastor is human and makes mistakes. No sin is greater than another. No matter what you have done, you can change.

The minute you make your mind up to do right by yourself, the enemy is waiting to attack

If God said that you are good enough, then no matter what you have done, He will wash you clean and throw it in the sea of forgetfulness. Why then should anyone else's opinion make you doubt your worth? Do you think those that are judging you are better than you? Do you think they have no sin? Be careful how you allow the opinions of others to place a muzzle on your story or hold you back from pursuing your dreams.

When God gives you a vision, He doesn't seek the approval of others. God will take you back to the town where you did the most dirt and use you to deliver a message. Why? Because those people in that town know your past. They will not let you forget your past. This will keep you humble. And when God blesses you in their face, they will know it was God, and He will get the glory. If God used someone who was unfamiliar, who had a better reputation and was better gifted, nobody would give Him the glory. But when He takes an impossible situation and performs a miracle, he has to do it in the presence of those who were convinced it was impossible.

We are overcome by the words of our testimony. Everything you went through and all the mistakes you have made will be used to give God glory if you truly repent and serve Him with your heart. You are not the only one that has done or experienced what you have. God needs people on His side that can relate to those who are experiencing the same things they passed through. It is our duty to carry one another in their time of need. If you are too ashamed to be transparent, you will not be able to connect with those that God sent you to liberate and help on your purpose-fueled journey.

If you have made peace with something bad that you went through, when someone tries to remind you of it, you won't feel the need to hide or constantly apologize. After showing your true repentance, and you accept the fact that the past does not define you; that the past is the past, and you can't change it, and you decide to change your future, the enemy can no longer use your past to keep you bound in shame. Then you can share your experiences with others without feeling less around them. Your transparency will begin to be used as a key to free others from the bondage of their shame because they will see that they are not worse than others and can change their decisions just like you did.

This meant that I had to face the shame of failing in my relationships. I got out of my pride, admitted that I was not making the best decisions for myself or my children, and I asked for forgiveness. I knew God was going to use this in my purpose to help others. At the time, others couldn't see my vision for grand success when I had repeatedly made bad choices. I had no credibility, but it didn't matter. I felt free from an abusive relationship, I knew God did it, and I wasn't going back. I felt closure. I pressed forward with the same excitement and determination to prove that I had changed. I was worthy of being believed in. I believed in myself and what God was doing through me.

I began keeping a journal and I really enjoyed writing. I found it therapeutic to write what I was feeling and going through. That was how I worked through the process. I repented and made a new commitment to God, then to myself, to forgive myself, to be a better mother, to read more, to love myself more, to do everything with purely good intentions, and not let anyone else ever hit me again. I promised myself to acknowledge the value of God by acknowledging my value and to impact as many as I could with hope and give them a reason to believe that they can change their lives too. Through God, I found my purpose and finally built and erected my own holy doors.

THE END